Cambridge Elements

Elements in Earth System Governance
edited by
Frank Biermann
Utrecht University
Aarti Gupta
Wageningen University
Michael Mason
London School of Economics and Political Science (LSE)

THE CARBON MARKET CHALLENGE

Preventing Abuse Through Effective Governance

Regina Betz
Zurich University of Applied Sciences

Axel Michaelowa
University of Zurich

Paula Castro
Zurich University of Applied Sciences

Raphaela Kotsch
University of Zurich and Zurich University of Applied Sciences

Michael Mehling
Massachusetts Institute of Technology and University of Strathclyde

Katharina Michaelowa
University of Zurich

Andrea Baranzini
University of Applied Sciences and Arts of Western Switzerland

CAMBRIDGE
UNIVERSITY PRESS

Shaftesbury Road, Cambridge CB2 8EA, United Kingdom

One Liberty Plaza, 20th Floor, New York, NY 10006, USA

477 Williamstown Road, Port Melbourne, VIC 3207, Australia

314–321, 3rd Floor, Plot 3, Splendor Forum, Jasola District Centre,
New Delhi – 110025, India

103 Penang Road, #05–06/07, Visioncrest Commercial, Singapore 238467

Cambridge University Press is part of Cambridge University Press & Assessment,
a department of the University of Cambridge.

We share the University's mission to contribute to society through the pursuit of
education, learning and research at the highest international levels of excellence.

www.cambridge.org
Information on this title: www.cambridge.org/9781009216470

DOI: 10.1017/9781009216500

First published 2022

A catalogue record for this publication is available from the British Library.

ISBN 978-1-009-21647-0 Paperback
ISSN 2631-7818 (online)
ISSN 2631-780X (print)

The Carbon Market Challenge

Preventing Abuse Through Effective Governance

Elements in Earth System Governance

DOI: 10.1017/9781009216500
First published online: September 2022

Regina Betz
Zurich University of Applied Sciences

Axel Michaelowa
University of Zurich

Paula Castro
Zurich University of Applied Sciences

Raphaela Kotsch
University of Zurich and Zurich University of Applied Sciences

Michael Mehling
Massachusetts Institute of Technology and University of Strathclyde

Katharina Michaelowa
University of Zurich

Andrea Baranzini
University of Applied Sciences and Arts of Western Switzerland

Author for correspondence: Paula Castro, paula.castro@zhaw.ch

Abstract: Carbon markets – both emissions trading systems and baseline-and-credit systems – are an increasingly common policy instrument being introduced to address climate change mitigation. However, their design is crucial to ensure that they deliver cost-effective emission reductions while maintaining environmental integrity. This Element puts together a comprehensive, principle-based overview of the risks and abuses to environmental integrity and cost effectiveness that have emerged for carbon markets at all jurisdictional levels around the world, provides concrete examples, and offers effective policy and governance solutions to overcome such risks. This title is also available as Open Access on Cambridge Core.

This Element also has a video abstract: www.cambridge.org/carbon_market

Keywords: carbon market, emissions trading system, climate policy, environmental integrity, cost effectiveness

ISBNs: 9781009216470 (PB), 9781009216500 (OC)
ISSNs: 2631-7818 (online), 2631-780X (print)

Contents

1 An Introduction to Carbon Markets

1.1 Relevance of Carbon Markets

How to address climate change is one of the greatest global governance problems of our time. At the international, national, and subnational levels, over 50 different carbon markets have been implemented as a key policy to incentivize the reduction of greenhouse gas (GHG) emissions in a cost-effective and flexible way, and several more are being planned or considered (World Bank, 2021). In addition, 89 Nationally Determined Contributions (NDCs) submitted by Parties to the 2015 Paris Agreement mention the use of carbon markets as a condition for achieving their mitigation targets (Pauw et al., 2016). Article 6 of the Paris Agreement envisages the implementation of carbon markets or similar international cooperative arrangements as a policy instrument to facilitate the achievement of its goals.

Carbon markets are markets where a certain amount of GHG (e.g., a tonne CO_2 equivalent) is commodified as a tradable unit either as an emission allowance issued under a cap-and-trade system or as a verified emission reduction/removal credit issued under a baseline-and-credit system.

In "cap-and-trade" or emissions trading systems (ETS), a regulator defines an allowed maximum level of GHG emissions (the "cap") for a certain group of entities (e.g., countries, companies, or facilities). The cap is then subdivided into distinct emission allowances, which are distributed to the regulated entities. The covered entities need to submit one allowance for each tonne of carbon dioxide equivalent (CO_2e) emitted during a compliance period, usually a year. The initial allocation of allowances to covered entities can be free of charge, e.g., based on historical emissions levels ("grandparenting"), partially free (with free allocation limited by a politically determined technology performance benchmark), and/or sold at auction by the regulator.

In a "baseline-and-credit" system a regulator[1] defines how emission (reduction or removal) credits can be generated by activities that reduce GHG emissions or remove GHGs from the atmosphere compared to a reference scenario (baseline) that reflects the counterfactual situation without these activities. The difference between the baseline emissions and the emissions of the activity determines how many credits can be issued. To generate emission credits, ex post verification of the reduction/removal by an officially recognized institution – a verifier – is necessary. The emission credits can then be used as offsets against mandatory or voluntary GHG emission targets or other

---

[1] In the context of voluntary carbon markets, private standard organizations can take up regulatory functions.

policy instruments aiming at GHG mitigation. Table 1 shows the key differences between a baseline-and-credit and a cap-and-trade system.

Both types of units form the supply in the market. There can be different types of demand for allowances or credits at different levels. Governments can use units to comply with emissions targets under an international treaty such as the Kyoto Protocol or the Paris Agreement. Companies can use allowances to comply with their targets under emissions trading schemes. In some jurisdictions, they can use credits in emissions trading systems, dedicated baseline-and-credit systems for specific sectors, or instead of having to pay carbon taxes (e.g., as allowed in Colombia or South Africa). Finally, private companies and individuals can use credits for offsetting emissions in the context of their voluntary GHG mitigation targets; such demand has increased significantly in the past years.

The carbon price is discovered in both compliance and voluntary markets through the buying and selling of units, whereas the scarcity of units and the marginal costs of reducing greenhouse gases influence the price. The initial allocation or issuance of allowances and credits by the regulatory authority represents the primary carbon market. Allowances and credits can then be traded in the secondary carbon markets (spot market), either directly between parties, usually facilitated by brokers (over-the-counter transactions, OTC), or traded on an exchange. While the latter requires prior standardization of contracts, for OTC transactions, the transacting parties can freely shape the contract in terms of, for example, price and volume of units being traded. Since the details of these contracts are generally not published, OTC transactions can be quite opaque for other market players and regulators (Kachi and Frerk, 2013). A further component of carbon markets is the derivative market. It is composed of financial instruments, such as options and futures contracts, to hedge the risks associated with emission allowances and credits.

We would like to note that, in practice, the terminology is not always used consistently. While the IPCC Assessment Reports (Gupta et al., 2007; Stavins et al., 2014) and all relevant carbon market research literature (e.g., Michaelowa et al., 2019b) apply the terms as defined in this volume, a few practitioners[2] further differentiate baseline-and-credit systems into those that use emission credits for offsetting and those (national or subnational) systems in which baseline emission levels are defined for individual regulated entities (e.g., based on historical levels or on an industry standard) and units are issued to entities that have reduced their emissions below this level. Under such a system, units can be sold only to other entities exceeding their baseline emission levels.

---

[2] See, e.g., the definitions by the World Bank under https://carbonpricingdashboard.worldbank.org/what-carbon-pricing.

Table 1 Differences between baseline-and-credit and cap-and-trade systems

Baseline-and-credit	Cap-and-trade
Emission reductions/removals compared to baseline or target are tradable	Allocated allowances, which allow holders to emit a certain quantity of emissions, are tradable
Units are credits and are generated *ex post* after verification (and certification)	Units are allowances and allocated/auctioned *ex ante* to regulated entities
Wide participation in unit generation	Tradable surplus of units can only be created by regulated entities
System needs to be integrated and linked to other types of policies such as a cap-and-trade system or carbon tax, or to corporate or individual voluntary mitigation targets	System needs own implementation
Examples:	Examples:
Clean Development Mechanism	Subnational, national, and supra-national emissions trading systems (such as the Californian, the Swiss, or the South Korean systems, or the EU ETS)
Joint Implementation	
The Article 6.4 Mechanism under the Paris Agreement	
Carbon Offsetting and Reduction Scheme for International Aviation	International emissions trading under Article 17 of the Kyoto Protocol
Voluntary carbon standards (e.g., Gold Standard, Verra)	

Source: Authors.

Following the research literature, in our volume we use the term "baseline-and-credit-system" in a broad sense, covering all types of markets in which emission credits are issued compared to a baseline. We also note that occasionally the literature uses the term "emissions trading" as an umbrella for all systems described above.

1.2 Carbon Markets Around the World

Currently, at least 29 ETS and 27 baseline-and-credit systems[3] are in place around the world, covering international, supranational, national, and subnational jurisdictions (World Bank, 2021).

---

[3] This excludes the voluntary market, where there are a few large, internationally relevant standards (Verra, Gold Standard) but a plethora of smaller standards, both internationally and domestically.

At the global level, the 1997 Kyoto Protocol to the UN Framework Convention on Climate Change (UNFCCC) introduced three market-based flexibility mechanisms: the Clean Development Mechanism (CDM), Joint Implementation (JI), and International Emissions Trading (IET). The CDM is a baseline-and-credit system that finances emission reduction projects in countries without emission reduction targets under the Kyoto Protocol (so-called non-Annex I countries). The Certified Emission Reductions (CERs) generated by these projects can be used by countries with targets under the Kyoto Protocol (Annex B countries) toward their own compliance. JI is a similar baseline-and-credit mechanism, which operates in Annex B countries. The units it generates are called Emission Reduction Units (ERUs). There are two forms of JI: Track 2, which is subject to international oversight, and Track 1, which is not. IET allows Annex B countries to trade the Kyoto Protocol's unused Assigned Allowance Units (AAUs) with each other.

Under its Article 6, the 2015 Paris Agreement specifies the implementation of similar market-based mechanisms, with detailed rules agreed by COP26 in 2021. Direct bilateral cooperation under Article 6.2 allows, for example, the linking of national, subnational, and supranational ETS and the trading of so-called Internationally Transferred Mitigation Outcomes (ITMOs) in a way comparable to IET and to JI Track 1 projects. A multilaterally overseen Article 6.4 Mechanism will be a baseline-and-credit system similar to CDM and JI Track 2 (Michaelowa et al., 2019c). In addition, in 2016, the International Civil Aviation Organization (ICAO) established a pilot baseline-and-credit mechanism known as CORSIA (Carbon Offsetting and Reduction Scheme for International Aviation). CORSIA, which started operating in 2021, aims to incentivize carbon-neutral growth of the international aviation sector.

At the supranational level, the EU ETS is the largest ETS currently in place. It covers installations in the power and heat generation, energy-intensive industry, and commercial aviation sectors in all 27 EU member states as well as Iceland, Liechtenstein, and Norway. It has set emissions limits for more than 11,000 installations and airlines, covering about 40 percent of the EU's GHG emissions.[4]

So far, eight national-level ETS are operating, and more are being planned. Subnationally, several Canadian, Chinese, Japanese, and US jurisdictions have implemented or are planning ETS. In addition, several of these jurisdictions have implemented baseline-and-credit systems to supply offsets to their ETS (ICAP, 2021; World Bank, 2021).

Figure 1 presents a simplified overview of the main international carbon markets, their linkages, and traded units.

---

[4] https://ec.europa.eu/clima/policies/ets_en.

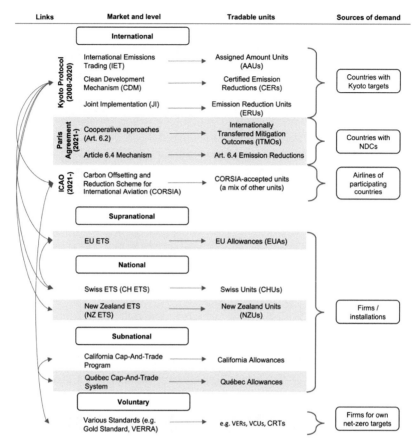

Figure 1 Examples of trading systems, linkages and traded units

Source: Own graphic. The red arrows depict direct links between the different systems which allow them to trade with each other. In addition to this, some markets may be linked indirectly – e.g., the EU ETS and the NZ ETS are connected through their link to the Kyoto Protocol mechanisms.

This volume does not aim to be comprehensive and cover all carbon markets but rather focuses on major compliance markets. For a comparison of national-level baseline-and-credit schemes see Michaelowa and colleagues (2019b), while an excellent overview of national emissions trading schemes has been done by Haites (2018). It also does not provide a comprehensive description of the political processes that led to the evolution (and improvement) of carbon markets over time (for this, see, e.g., Wettestad and Jevnaker, 2016, 2019; Michaelowa et al., 2019c). Rather, its goal is to focus on the risks that surround the design of carbon markets and the solutions that have been devised to address those risks. Instead of offering full case studies of individual carbon markets, then, we use them to derive lessons across the various design aspects of carbon markets.

1.3 Carbon Markets as Polycentric Governance Arrangements

Carbon markets are complex governance arrangements (see Ahonen et al., 2022). They entail artificially created markets for goods – emission allowances or credits – that are created by policy. As described above, they have emerged at all levels of governance, and engage public and private actors in regulatory and governance functions. They comprise various, mostly independent governance systems that are interlinked – in a few cases through formal market links, but in most cases loosely through flows of information and expertise, capacity building, and through the overarching goal of helping to achieve international climate mitigation commitments (Burtraw et al., 2013; Paterson et al., 2014; Biedenkopf et al., 2017). For these reasons, carbon markets are inherently polycentric in nature, involving multiple and often overlapping sources of authority (Jordan et al., 2018).

When the sources of authority cross the boundaries between different levels of public and private governance, the literature speaks of transnational governance. As early as in 2008, the CDM was portrayed by Pattberg and Stripple (2008) as a prototype of this form of governance; the Article 6.4 mechanism under the Paris Agreement is comparable. At the UNFCCC level, the parties adopt political guidance, whereas the Supervisory Body takes care of day-to-day decision-making. At the national level, state-appointed Designated National Authorities approve potential Article 6.4 activities in the host country. Private entities – so-called Designated Operational Entities (DOEs) – validate and verify the activities and their baseline methodologies (see Figure 2). Further private actors are involved in identifying, proposing, and investing in activities. Some of them also help to shape the rules and regulations that govern this market. Finally, multilateral organizations, including through public–private partnerships, provide technical advisory, capacity building, and project finance. Under the CDM this was done by the World Bank's Prototype Carbon Fund; more recently, the World Bank Partnership for Market Readiness took up a similar role.

The EU ETS involves much authority at the supranational level, along with the national level, with a deep intertwining of decision-makers at both levels, and an additional involvement of private actors (Bailey and Maresh, 2009). The balance of authority exercised by the supranational and the national levels – for instance, in terms of allocation of allowances – has important implications for the environmental effectiveness of the system (Clò, 2009).

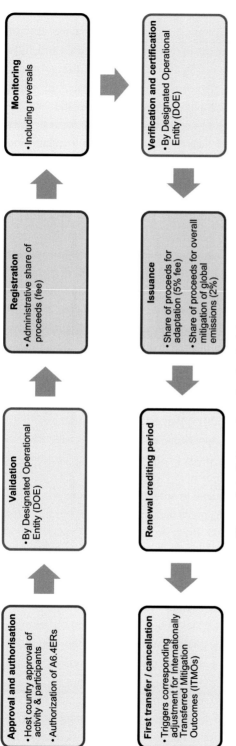

Figure 2 Activity cycle under the Article 6.4 mechanism

Source: Own graphic.

Note: A6.4ERs = Article 6.4 Emission Reductions (tradeable units under Art. 6.4); SOP = Share of proceeds (tax for financing adaptation and administration). Colors denote the actors involved in the process.

In addition, the voluntary carbon market represents an extreme case of involvement of private actors as sources of governance. In words still fully adequate today, Pattberg and Stripple (2008: 378) described the voluntary carbon market as "a site of climate governance beyond the state," in which various, mostly private, actors compete in developing validation and verification standards and providing offsets of varying qualities. Over the last years some large voluntary carbon market standards such as Gold Standard and partially Verra have become more stringent than international compliance markets like the CDM, while small niche standards have offered low-quality credits (Ahonen et al., 2022).

Governance arrangements for carbon markets, therefore, exemplify a much broader trend in global environmental governance, away from traditional state-centered multilateral regimes, and toward a co-existence with private and hybrid forms of governance in which new types of actors exhibit authority, experiment with novel arrangements and policy instruments, and interact at various jurisdictional levels (Pattberg and Stripple, 2008; Biermann, 2010). In the past decade, these complex multilevel, and polycentric, arrangements have been extensively researched in terms of their implications for effectiveness, institutional interaction, policy learning, diffusion, and convergence, as well as the role of local cultures, ideology, and political economic factors in shaping them (for the case of carbon markets see, e.g., Clò, 2009; Wettestad, 2009; Knox-Hayes, 2016; Biedenkopf et al., 2017; Wettestad and Gulbrandsen, 2018).

These novel arrangements entail opportunities but also risks for climate governance and its effectiveness. In terms of opportunities, carbon markets are characterized by a strong degree of policy experimentation and learning (Biedenkopf et al., 2017), which can lead to solutions that will, over time, be better for the climate. At the same time, given the increasingly decentralized (or "fragmented," see Biermann et al., 2009; Biedenkopf et al., 2017) authority, it is likely that these arrangements will lead to insufficient, patchy, and uncoordinated regulation that may result in regulatory loopholes and abuses. Misaligned interests and resources between the different sides involved in policymaking may further increase these risks (see, e.g., Bailey and Maresh, 2009).

It is, therefore, crucial to take a closer look at how these governance arrangements perform in terms of regulatory quality, and what risks they entail for ensuring environmental integrity and improving economic efficiency.

Contrary to what policy diffusion theory would predict, there has been a high degree of divergence in market design as policymakers have learned from the mistakes of previous experiences, and as they have adapted existing designs to the structural and political particularities of their own jurisdictions (Biedenkopf et al., 2017; Wettestad and Gulbrandsen, 2018). This has led to great variation in the regulatory and design aspects of carbon markets (Gulbrandsen et al., 2019).

In a context in which we now have substantial experience with various carbon markets at different levels, but where many new markets are being planned, there is a need to survey these various market design characteristics, identify where there are risks for environmental integrity and economic efficiency, and propose lessons for future policy design, with a particular emphasis on sound regulatory oversight. That is what this volume seeks to achieve.

2 Toward a Principle-Based Assessment of Regulatory Frameworks for Carbon Markets

How can we evaluate carbon market design options in a systematic and objective way? Carbon markets are created through political processes to achieve climate policy goals. For this reason, they must comply with legal, economic, and environmental principles generally associated with policy instruments, or more specifically related to the creation and functioning of a market. In the following sections, we rely on such principles to assess the potential abuses and broader risks to environmental integrity and economic efficiency that may emerge in the design and implementation of baseline-and-credit and cap-and-trade systems and the related trading activities, to discuss the performance of regulatory frameworks used in existing markets, and to collect lessons for mitigating those risks and preventing abuses.

We consider market abuses to consist of any action by an individual, group, or company to exploit the market to their own advantage in a way that can affect environmental integrity or economic efficiency. With risks we denote the likelihood that such abuses may take place, including lobbying efforts which lead to rules reducing environmental integrity or efficiency. Abuses may be the unintended consequence of regulatory loopholes – something likely to happen in international and multilevel markets where several, not necessarily consistent, bodies of law may apply. But they can also include illegal and even criminal practices.

Examples include traditional market abuses such as price manipulation, money laundering, collusion, cyber-attacks, and other predatory behavior, and carbon-market-specific abuses such as misreporting of performance data to increase the number of credits issued. Risks include design risks related to lax cap-setting or other crucial design elements such as sanctions or monitoring, reporting, and verification rules. For each risk or abuse, we offer a description, assess its relevance, offer real-life examples, and suggest tools for its prevention, detection, and enforcement.

2.1 Legal Principles for Carbon Markets

Generally, principles are variously understood as a "fundamental truth or doctrine," "a proposition so clear that it cannot be proved or contradicted unless by a proposition which is still clearer," "that which constitutes the essence of a body or its constituent parts," and "that which pertains to the theoretical part of a science" (Black, 1990: 1193). Their scope, therefore, is vague and abstract. In a legal context, however, principles acquire a narrower, more formal role and can take on specific legal effects.

Principles are an integral part of most legal systems and considered necessary for their functioning, without necessarily being set out in written law (Kohen and Schramm, 2013). Their normativity may derive from long-standing practice and legal custom or from accepted requirements of fairness and justice (Dworkin, 1978). Sometimes, however, legal principles are also expressly set out in treaty instruments, statutory law, or even constitutions.

Although the existence of legally relevant principles is hardly disputed, their exact role and definition remain a matter of continued jurisprudential debate. Their legal scope is generally acknowledged to be general and abstract. They apply to a broad and unspecified set of actors and situations which can include future and as yet unknown circumstances or transactions.

They are thus distinct from rules, which are more binary in nature and call for an automatic outcome whenever specified conditions are met (Dworkin, 1978). Principles do not involve such an automatism. Rather, their role is often seen as subsidiary. They guide administrative discretion or judicial decisions where legal rules allow for different outcomes, due to textual ambiguity, the existence of substantive gaps, or conflicts between different applicable rules (Kohen and Schramm, 2013). As a result, legal principles rarely have the normative force to decide a dispute or determine a legal question on their own. They tend to require further elaboration through legislation, case law, or scholarly writing to take effect.

Several legal principles may be relevant for the regulation of carbon trading. It would be difficult – if not impossible – to enumerate all of them, however. Across legal systems and jurisdictions, and even across different areas of law, countless principles of varying weight and degrees of conceptual clarity exist, with sometimes subtle differences in terminology and material substance. We consider selected key principles of public law, private law, and the cross-cutting substantive area of environmental law to potentially be the most relevant ones.

2.1.1 Principles of Public Law

With regard to public law, a vast majority of legal systems based on the rule of law recognize certain general principles that govern the exercise of public authority and constrain government power. These include the principles of legality, *nulla poena sine lege*, proportionality, effectiveness, equivalence, equality, and subsidiarity.

2.1.2 Principles of Private Law

Transactions of goods and services, as well as other contractual relationships – including the transfer of emission allowances and credits – are usually governed by private law. Several principles have relevance for the validity and enforceability of such contractual relationships and transactions. These include the principles of good faith and estoppel, the abstraction principle, and *volenti non fit iniuria*.

2.1.3 Principles of Environmental Law

Carbon markets are an instrument of climate policy, and their primary goal is typically the achievement of GHG mitigation objectives at reduced economic cost. Climate policy, in turn, has historically evolved from environmental policy. This means that many doctrines and principles of environmental law may be relevant to carbon markets. These include the principle of common, but differentiated, responsibilities (CBDR, also in a variation including "and respective capabilities"), the precautionary principle and the polluter-pays principle.

Table 2 explains these principles and describes their potential relevance for carbon markets.

2.1.4 Principles of Financial Market Regulation

Financial market regulation pursues several objectives: to maintain market confidence, contribute to the stability of the financial system, and secure an appropriate degree of consumer protection. In this context, a principle-based approach is sometimes discussed as adherence to the spirit of financial market regulation rather than its precise wording. Although financial market regulation tends to follow general tenets such as transparency, efficiency, and stability, these are not legal principles in the sense described here. Instead, they are discussed in the next section on environmental and economic principles for carbon markets.

2.2 Environmental and Economic Principles for Carbon Markets

In an environmental and economic context, principles are more widely understood as a "moral rule or standard of good behavior,"[5] which is distinct from the more formal legal principles described in the previous section. In this section,

---

[5] https://dictionary.cambridge.org/us/dictionary/english/principle.

Table 2 Legal principles with potential relevance for carbon markets

Principle	Description	Relevance for carbon markets
Principles of public law		
Principle of legality (statutory reservation)	Administrative action can only be taken if and to the extent that it can be based on a legal mandate.	Potentially relevant, for instance, to the elaboration of any new carbon market rules, which require a prior legal basis to be adopted and applied.
Nulla poena sine lege	Criminal punishment can only be exacted for acts expressly prohibited by law.	Potentially relevant, for instance, to criminal sanctions imposed against violations of carbon market rules.
Principle of proportionality	The exercise of public authority has to pursue a legitimate purpose, be suited and necessary to achieve that purpose, and achieve a reasonable balance between competing legal interests.	Potentially relevant, for instance, to any carbon market rules that narrow the rights and freedoms of market participants.
Principle of effectiveness	A set of rules has to, by and large, command observance and see enforcement to have a claim to validity. (Not to be confounded with outcome-related effectiveness discussed below under environmental integrity.)	Potentially relevant to any carbon market rules that have been elaborated on paper but are not applied and enforced.
Principle of equivalence	Any fees and charges imposed by public authorities need to be proportionate to the service provided.	Potentially relevant, for instance, to any fees charged from carbon market participants for market access and participation.
Principle of equality/ non-discrimination	In exercising public authority, discrimination or arbitrary distinction between otherwise equal subjects must be avoided.	Potentially relevant for any oversight or market access rules that distinguish between different categories of market participants without sufficient material justification.

Principle of subsidiarity	Social and political issues should be dealt with at the most immediate (or local) level consistent with resolving them.	Potentially relevant for determining the level of governance at which issues related to the carbon market should be regulated.
Principles of private law		
Principle of good faith	The parties to a contract will deal with each other honestly and fairly, so as not to undermine the right of the other party or parties to receive the benefits of the contract.	Potentially relevant for questions of ownership and title in the event of a transfer of allowances or credits obtained through prior fraud or an otherwise faulty transaction.
Principle of estoppel	Legal subjects are restrained from asserting a particular position in law where it would be inequitable to do so, for instance due to prior behavior and the legitimate expectation resulting therefrom.	Potentially relevant for, e.g., retroactive cancellation or rejection of allowances or credits due to security or integrity concerns where prior administrative practice has led holders to expect a different outcome.
Abstraction principle	The contractual arrangement underlying a transaction is separate from the actual conveyance of title to transacted goods or rights.	Potentially relevant for any carbon market rules that affect or prevent transfer of title, even where a valid purchase contract has been signed.
Volenti non fit iniuria	When someone willingly and knowingly places themselves in a position of risk, they are not able to bring a claim against another party in tort or delict.	Potentially relevant for situations involving transfers of faulty allowances or credits.

Table 2 (cont.)

Principle	Description	Relevance for carbon markets
Principles of environmental law		
Common but differentiated responsibilities (and respective capabilities)	All states have a shared obligation to address environmental degradation but without equal responsibility of all states for that degradation, which justifies differentiated commitments.	Potentially relevant for any governance rules applicable to international carbon markets involving both developed and developing countries.
Precautionary principle	Defines the appropriate timing and scope of measures against uncertain environmental risks, justifying action even in the presence of scientific uncertainty when the potential harm of inaction is great.	Potentially relevant to justify regulatory safeguards to ensure carbon market integrity even where the exact nature and scale of risk – e.g., of abuse – remain uncertain.
Polluter-pays principle	Derived from economic theory and the Pigouvian notion that market failures due to externalities such as environmental pollution can be corrected by imposing the corresponding social cost on the private actor causing that externality, thereby internalizing its social cost into the private cost of the underlying behavior.	Potential relevance in carbon market governance, inter alia, for the justification of policy intervention in the first place, and for sufficiently stringent rules to ensure integrity of emission allowances and credits.

Source: Authors.

we therefore define and describe the main environmental and economic principles that will guide our assessment of carbon markets and lay out some design elements that have an impact on those principles. Table 3 lists and describes these elements and their potential impact and points out to the sections of this volume where they are addressed.

2.2.1 Environmental Integrity

The principle of environmental integrity generally entails a "healthy natural system that can support essential processes" (Payne, 2017: 42), and is explicitly mentioned in Article 6.2 of the Paris Agreement, which will have growing relevance for carbon markets in the future.

For the case of carbon markets, different standards of environmental integrity can be conceived. Following Schneider and La Hoz Theuer (2019), we consider that environmental integrity is achieved when carbon markets do not lead to an increase in global aggregate emissions, compared to a situation without the carbon market. However, other interpretations of environmental integrity imply that carbon markets must achieve even *greater* mitigation than without them, and therefore contribute to increasing ambition. Economists often use the term "environmental effectiveness" when they refer to achieving such a positive environmental outcome. "Environmental integrity" is a broader term that also implies that the GHG abatement is correctly accounted for, and that it is not recorded as a reduction by two or more regulated entities simultaneously, thus avoiding double counting. As can be seen in Table 3, environmental integrity needs to be safeguarded across a range of design elements of these markets.

2.2.2 Economic Efficiency

In economic terms, the global climate is a *public good* and the adverse effects of GHG emissions constitute a negative externality to society since those who cause GHG emissions do not fully pay the costs of their contribution to climate change. This leads to a level of emissions that is socially suboptimal (i.e., inefficient). The polluter-pays principle mentioned above addresses the same issue. One way to react to this market failure is to establish a carbon price.

Imposing a carbon price that reflects the societal damage implied by the emissions leads polluters to consider the social cost in their private optimization. They will hence reduce emissions up to the point where the carbon price is equal to the marginal benefit of abatement (benefit from avoiding one additional unit of GHG emissions) and the marginal abatement cost (cost of reducing one additional unit of GHG emissions). However, the abatement costs vary by

Table 3 Environmental and economic principles with relevance for carbon markets, and related design elements

Design element	Description and impact	Relevance for carbon markets
Principle of environmental integrity		
Baseline	The baseline is the emissions level used as a benchmark for assessing the reductions achieved by a project; the more conservative the baseline, the higher the environmental integrity.	Relevant for baseline-and-credit systems; see Section 3.2.
Additionality testing	An emission reduction project is additional if it would not have taken place without the incentive generated by the carbon market. Additionality tests assess financial attractiveness of the activity.	Relevant for baseline-and-credit systems; see Section 3.3.
Crediting period	The crediting period refers to how long an activity is entitled to claim emission reductions; if an activity (e.g., a wind power plant) has a projected lifetime of 30 years but only credits emission reductions for 10 years, then it will generate more reductions than those accounted for in the market, increasing environmental integrity.	Relevant for baseline-and-credit systems; not further discussed in this volume.
Cap stringency	The cap is the quantity of emissions allowed for a system or an entity within a cap-and-trade system; the lower (more stringent) the cap, the higher the environmental integrity.	Relevant for cap-and-trade systems; see Section 4.1.
Treatment of permanence	Approaches to prevent or deal with reversal of emission reductions or removals achieved by an activity. These can include temporary credits, buffer reserves or tonne-year accounting.	Relevant for overshooting the cap when covering activities related to land-use, land-use change, and forestry; see Sections 4.2 and 5.1.

Sanctioning	Effective sanctions for noncompliance provide incentives to invest in reductions, buy allowances in cap-and-trade systems, or follow the rules of baseline-and-credit systems.	Relevant for overshooting the cap when sanctions are not effective; see Section 4.2.
Prevention of leakage	Leakage refers to the displacement of emissions or emitting activities to places outside the scope of the carbon market. Avoiding leakage is necessary to ensure that emission reductions actually take place.	Primarily relevant for cap-and-trade systems as a result of perverse incentives; see Section 4.3.
Revenue earmarking	Refers to how any revenues from the auctioning of emission allowances or the issuance of emission credits are used; if such revenues are (partly) earmarked for financing further mitigation projects, then they will increase environmental integrity.	Relevant for both cap-and-trade and baseline-and-credit systems; discussed here in the context of perverse incentives for state-owned firms; see Section 4.3.
Accounting rules	The rules for accounting emission or emission reduction units (i.e., reduction credits or emission allowances) need to make sure that these units are counted toward the fulfilment of only one emission reduction obligation (no double counting).	Relevant for all types of carbon markets, particularly when they are linked; see Section 5.2.
Principle of economic efficiency		
Coverage	The larger the emissions coverage and the more heterogeneous the actors covered, the greater the cost dispersion of the available abatement options which will result in higher efficiency gains from trading. Therefore, any increase in the sources or gases covered will increase efficiency and, additionally, enhance price stability and improve market liquidity.	Relevant for overshooting the cap under cap-and-trade systems; see Section 4.2.

Table 3 (cont.)

Design element	Description and impact	Relevance for carbon markets
Banking and borrowing rules	To ensure economic efficiency over time, regulated entities need to be able to save unused credits or allowances for future use or trade.	Relevant for the trading phase; discussed here in the context of the risk of surplus accumulation, which can increase when banking is allowed; see Section 4.1.
Transparency and reporting	To ensure liquidity and a proper price signal, markets require clear and frequent information about emissions, allowance allocation, surrender, and compliance; this allows efficient decisions by market participants.	Relevant for all markets and phases; discussed mainly in Section 5.1 on monitoring, reporting, and verification, but also in Sections 5.3, 5.4, 6.1, and 6.2.
Homogeneity of units	The more homogeneous (i.e., fungible) the units are, the greater the ease of trading, which increases liquidity and may support price discovery.	Relevant for the trading phase; see Section 5.1.
Principle of market stability		
Prevention of manipulation	Manipulation of the market price jeopardizes market stability and its economic efficiency.	Relevant for the trading phase; see Section 5.3.
Long-term legislation	Commitments to climate policy need to be accompanied by appropriate legislation to be credible and to provide long-term signaling.	Relevant for both types of markets; discussed mainly in Section 6.1 on lessons learned.
Institutional design	The introduction and implementation of an ETS requires high-quality institutions and governance; policies and systems need to be designed to be well adapted to existing institutional constraints.	Relevant for cap-and-trade and baseline-and-credit systems.

Principles of equity and fairness

Allocation method	Distributing emission allowances implies assigning property rights on the environment; free allocation grants a free rent to GHG emitters, while auctioning allowances implies that the atmosphere belongs to the community and is in line with the polluter-pays principle.	Relevant for cap-and-trade systems, discussed in the context of perverse incentives (but not explicitly in relation to equity and fairness) in Section 4.3.
Redistribution of revenues	Using the revenues generated through auctioning to decrease existing taxes or to finance public expenditures directly targeted to specific households can reduce inequalities and/or poverty.	Relevant mainly for cap-and-trade systems, not covered in this volume.
Geographical coverage	If the distribution of offsetting systems has a balanced geographical distribution, it can, for example, support energy sector development in poorer geographical areas.	Relevant mainly for baseline-and-credit systems; not covered in this volume.

Source: Authors.

technology. A functioning carbon market unfolds when emission reductions can be traded so that abatement takes place where it is cheapest.

However, in practice, the level of the carbon price depends on political decisions about the design of the market. The lower the cap, the more ambitious the baseline, and the fewer the offsets allowed, the higher the carbon price, which leads to a stronger incentive for behavioral changes toward reducing emissions (see Sections 4.1 and 4.2; for appropriate additionality and baseline determination under baseline-and-credit systems, see Sections 3.2 and 3.3; and for the trading phase, see in particular Section 5.3). The price may also be influenced if a participant possesses market power, which means that he/she can influence the carbon price unilaterally. In a thin market, with an insufficient supply of allowances, transactions are infrequent or nonexistent and the risk of market power is higher. These issues are addressed in Section 5.3 on market manipulation during the trading phase.

Efficiency needs to be seen from a dynamic perspective. A successful emissions trading system provides a clear and credible long-term price signal that mobilizes investments in low-carbon technologies and triggers behavioral changes toward sustainability. This is crucial for avoiding lock-in into high-carbon technologies and infrastructure, and for creating a continuous incentive to reduce emissions and to invest in the development, innovation, and diffusion of low-carbon technologies necessary to reach long-term reduction targets at the least possible cost.

2.2.3 Market Stability

Unpredictable or sudden shifts in rules and regulations affecting existing mechanisms lead to price volatility, impair the decision-making of market participants, and obstruct the long-term transition to low-carbon technologies. Market stability is therefore crucial to building trust and credibility in the emissions trading system. Yet, this relationship is reciprocal and market stability also depends on the trust and credibility of the market.

2.2.4 Equity and Fairness

Equity can be interpreted in different ways. We emphasize here the social dimensions of climate policies, focusing on the conditions under which carbon markets do not increase (and may even decrease) poverty or inequality. While efficiency only requires that the social costs of pollution be considered, equity and fairness dictate who should shoulder those costs, namely the polluters. This again refers to the polluter-pays principle and requires specific policies regarding the allocation of allowances or the redistribution of costs and benefits.

The goals of equity and fairness are also related to the broader principle of sustainable development including social and economic improvements beyond environmental benefits. A detailed discussion is, however, beyond the scope of this volume.

The next sections discuss the role of selected principles and design elements more specifically. We first focus on baseline-and-credit systems, for which the risk of inefficiency and low effectiveness or abuse is more decentralized and relevant for individual projects and the emission reduction credits they generate. For cap-and-trade systems, on the other hand, those risks are more centralized and related to the overall design of the system, as design features, such as the number of allowances or rules about exemptions and market oversight, have a much higher impact on efficiency and effectiveness and the possibility of abuse.

3 Baseline-and-Credit Systems

Given that most players directly involved in baseline-and-crediting mechanisms have an incentive to overstate the generated number of credits, there is a high likelihood that environmental integrity is at risk. On the one hand, activity developers benefit from getting a larger credit volume and can exploit information asymmetries (Strand and Rosendahl, 2012; Chen et al., 2021). In a large market, the effect of lowering credit prices due to increased supply cannot be influenced by each single market participant, so each participant will want to maximize their credits. On the other hand, credit buyers acquire a larger supply of credits at lower prices, so they are also interested in larger credit volumes. Host country governments benefit from larger credit sales unless they must apply a "corresponding adjustment" to their own mitigation achievements for the volume sold. The only group of players that will unequivocally oppose inflated numbers of credits are environmental NGOs.

Under such circumstances, almost all players will lobby for laxer rules in order to maximize the amount of credits generated. Voluntary markets are particularly susceptible to even laxer rules as corresponding adjustments to reduce the over-crediting incentive are not mandatory and there may be less oversight by central institutions. It seems, therefore, that the risk of abuses of baseline-and-credit systems is higher in voluntary carbon markets compared to regulated markets.

3.1 Characteristics of Baseline-and-Credit Systems and Possibilities for Abuse

Two main criteria are typically considered when assessing the quality of a baseline-and-credit system: additionality and setting an appropriate baseline.

Both are key to ensuring environmental integrity, and both, therefore, offer the greatest risk for abuse and damage to the environment.

"Additionality" refers to whether a project, for instance an investment in a more efficient production process, is actually mobilized by the revenue coming from emission credit sales, or whether the investment would have happened anyway. If a project is viable even without the incentive of selling credits, then it is not additional. If non-additional activities are accepted under a mechanism, the cost of credit generation will be zero or even negative. Players with non-additional activities can, therefore, sell credits at any price that covers the transaction costs for credit generation. In this case, the credit volume will increase while the price will decrease.

The other main risk for abuse is related to how baseline emissions levels are set (Michaelowa, 2005). Abuse in the context of baseline setting means that baseline emissions levels are set at a higher level than would be the case if the baseline had been specified in line with environmental integrity. Such abuse can be undertaken by governments or activity developers and happen in different ways, including through the use of manipulated data or by increasing emissions beforehand to achieve higher reductions later (see Section 3.2.1). Compared to a situation with correct baselines, the volume of credits will increase. If the credit demand does not change, the equilibrium price for credits will decrease.

In both cases, the extra credit volume generated does not represent a real reduction in emissions. If the credits are used for compliance under a cap-and-trade system, the stringency of the cap will de facto be reduced by this extra credit volume and more emissions will be released into the atmosphere compared to a situation without the possibility of surrendering credits.

Regulators have long been aware of the risks of baseline and additionality abuse and have applied different approaches to address them. Under the Kyoto mechanisms CDM and JI, as well as the voluntary carbon market standards Gold Standard and Verra, validation of project documentation by third-party auditors is mandatory. This validation aims to provide an independent audit and to uncover cases where data used to argue additionality are manipulated. Auditors need to be accredited with the regulators to ensure that their quality is sufficient. However, the fact that validators have an interest in being hired again by project/program developers generates a disincentive to check documentation too carefully. If a validator rejects a validation, the program developer is less likely to hire the validator in the future. This disincentive is particularly strong if the project development is undertaken by highly specialized companies, as was the case under the CDM. A similar disincentive applies for verification of emission reductions achieved by projects, especially if verifications are frequent. These disincentives could be eliminated by random allocation of validators and verifiers to projects by the regulators. Such an approach would require the definition of a common fee scale for validation and verification to prevent excessive fees. The New South Wales Greenhouse Gas Abatement Scheme (GGAS), which ran from 2003 to 2012, followed this approach, requiring that the regulating authority was the client of the third-party verifiers and validators.

There is a surprisingly small amount of academic literature empirically addressing these risks. Drew and Drew (2010) provided a first rough general overview of fraud under the CDM. Only very recently, Chen and colleagues (2021) have published a highly elaborate empirical study assessing over 2000 CDM projects regarding additionality fraud. This study is discussed in detail below.

3.2 Risks Related to Baseline Setting

Baseline methodologies differ significantly across baseline-and-credit mechanisms. The Kyoto mechanisms CDM and JI have approved over 250 methodologies, while other mechanisms, such as the Joint Crediting Mechanism (JCM), and mechanisms under voluntary market standards, such as the Gold Standard and Verified Carbon Standard (VCS), add another 50 methodologies.

Under the CDM, three principal approaches for baseline setting were applied: historical emissions levels, emissions levels of an economically attractive course of action, and the best 10 percent of comparable technology (benchmark approach).

In many baseline methodologies, the correct estimation of the duration during which a technology is effectively used within a typical week (or month) plays an important role. Overestimation of usage duration increases baseline emissions and generates upwardly biased estimates of emission reductions.

Rosendahl and Strand (2009) and Strand and Rosendahl (2012) stressed the asymmetric information available to project developers and regulators that favors the former and leads to systemic overestimates of baselines.

3.2.1 Examples

The key discussions about baseline fraud relate to perverse incentives to increase emissions levels beyond historical levels in order to maximize emission credit sales revenues. Strictly speaking, this is not baseline fraud but manipulation of a project activity. This risk is seen as particularly high whenever the revenues from the sale of products are lower than those from the emissions credits. This is the case for projects to destroy HFC-23 gas, a by-product of the production of the refrigerant HCFC-22. Schneider (2011) clearly showed that such projects maximize HFC-23 production levels until the maximum level to be credited is reached, lowering them once the threshold is exceeded.

Simple fraud regarding baselines would relate to applying a baseline methodology correctly but feeding it with manipulated data. For example, the carbon content of baseline fuels could be exaggerated, especially for fuels such as coal that have a wide quality range. Fraud could include submitting samples with a particularly high carbon content to the laboratory or faking a laboratory report. There is no published example of baseline fuel emission coefficient fraud, nor has such fraud been informally discussed within the expert community. But in the context of cap-and-trade systems there is some anecdotal evidence that the sampling has been biased in order to increase free allocation or reduce surrendering requirements (Section 5.1).

The most problematic case of baseline-setting abuse is the "laundering" of "hot air" by governments. Hot air refers to emissions credits generated by applying overestimated baselines, which consider emission reductions due to the economic downturn in Russia, Ukraine, and Eastern Europe in the 1990s as if they had been reached through active mitigation policies.

Hot air laundering can even go beyond baseline fraud by inventing fictitious projects. When it became likely in early 2012 that the direct sale of hot air would be prohibited for the second commitment period of the Kyoto Protocol, Ukraine and Russia resorted to approving Track 1 JI projects with spuriously high baselines. The detailed analysis by Kollmuss and colleagues (2015) shows that Ukraine alone registered 78 projects aimed at preventing spontaneous ignition of coal piles in the Eastern Ukrainian coal basin, generating 219 million credits. Seventy-four of these were only approved once the outcomes of the UNFCCC Subsidiary Body meetings in late May 2012 suggested that direct sales of hot air would soon be prohibited (Figure 3). This project type has not been submitted to any other baseline-and-credit mechanism elsewhere since it would surely have been rejected. Baseline manipulation of these projects has two components: the assumption that 78–83 percent of the coal in the waste pile would burn, and that this would happen exactly during the years 2008–2012 (Kollmuss et al., 2015: 46). In reality, much less coal would burn, and the fires would be spread out over a very long period.

Given the economic downturn in the 1990s, country-level emissions were much lower than the wrongly determined country-level baseline (all the hot air), so that Ukraine could sell a high number of credits from these Track 1 JI projects and still meet its Kyoto Protocol commitments. The example shows how politically ill-conceived country-level baselines and manipulated project-level baselines together lead to the laundering of hot air.

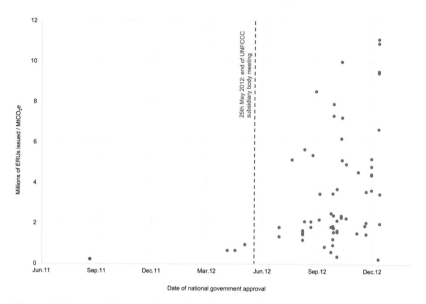

Figure 3 Approval dates and credit volumes of Ukrainian coal pile JI projects
Source: Own graph, adapted from Kollmuss and colleagues (2015: 45). The red dot indicates the only Track 2 coal pile project; all others are Track 1 projects.

A less blatant, but still relevant, baseline manipulation was undertaken by Russia for projects reducing flaring of associated petroleum gas, where the baseline emissions intensity was set at almost double the level that is shown in the national emissions inventory (Kollmuss et al., 2015: 57).

3.2.2 Prevention, Detection, and Enforcement

Baselines should never be set by the entity that benefits from credit sales without a third-party validation. To avoid conflicts of interest, regulatory authorities, rather than project developers, should commission verifiers or validators. In addition, regulators should check regularly for unusual patterns in the performance of approved projects/programs that could indicate manipulation of baselines. Ex post detection of unusual effects by the regulators such as the one uncovered by Schneider (2011) should lead to the rejection of future credit issuance. Previously issued credits should not be canceled to avoid creating uncertainty on the part of the buyer, but the project developer, having sold these credits, should have to buy and cancel a volume of credits to make good on the past manipulation.

3.3 Risks Related to Additionality Determination

Additionality determination has been addressed most thoroughly under the CDM. The CDM started with the approach to assess whether a project faces barriers which could be overcome due to the CDM status of the project. This approach was severely criticized by researchers (Schneider, 2009) and NGOs alike, for instance when WikiLeaks dug up a cable from U.S. diplomats in India citing a number of Indian businessmen stating that the "CDM incentive is a 'bonus' but not the 'driver' of business operations."[6] As a result, CDM regulators no longer accepted a barrier argumentation but required an investment test as proposed by Greiner and Michaelowa (2003). Over time, the investment test became more refined, and key parameters such as threshold values for internal rates of return (IRR) were prescribed (Michaelowa, 2009). Chen and colleagues (2021) showed that this substantially reduced the scope for manipulation.

After the prices of CDM credits fell significantly in 2012–2013 and project developers complained about the prohibitive costs of the investment tests, positive lists of activities automatically considered additional gained ground under the CDM. They were first applied for micro-scale activities and later also for small- and large-scale activities. While positive lists cannot be manipulated, they generate loopholes for certain activities at the margin of categories covered by the list or in sectors with dynamic technological development and reductions of investment cost (Hayashi and Michaelowa, 2013). For example, grid-connected solar PV installations of just below 15 MW are highly attractive commercially in many countries but still qualify under the positive list.

Michaelowa and colleagues (2019a) discussed how to prevent manipulation of additionality determination when international carbon markets under Article 6 of the Paris Agreement allow the generation of emission credits from the introduction of policy instruments. The higher the carbon price generated by such an instrument, the higher the share of mitigation that goes beyond business as usual will be. Therefore, Michaelowa and colleagues (2019a) proposed carbon price benchmarks for policy instruments to qualify, differentiated by country groups. For example, a carbon tax would have to exceed USD 5/tCO_2 in a developing country context to qualify for crediting.

3.3.1 Examples

A common way of manipulating additionality determination used by renewable electricity generation activities is to underestimate the load factor of the power plant. Such an underestimation shows lower electricity sales and hence lower revenues than actually achieved and results in a downward bias of the IRR. In a similar fashion, prices for inputs such as agricultural residues for biomass power plants can be overestimated to make the project activity appear less attractive.

---

[6] https://wikileaks.org/plusd/cables/08MUMBAI340_a.html.

The Aquarius hydro project in Brazil (CDM Registration No. 0627) estimated a plant load factor of 70 percent in its project documentation. De facto, the load factors reached between 89 and 95 percent in the years 2007 to 2010, as shown by the monitoring reports (CDM Executive Board, 2011a).

In a study commissioned by CDM regulators, Meng (2013) compared projected with actual load factors in 150 wind power projects and found that the projected load factor had been underestimated in 22 percent of these projects.

Another frequently used approach to reduce the IRR is the use of company-internal transfer pricing to make project outlays look higher than they actually are. For example, in a waste-gas-fired power plant in the JSW Vijayanagar steel mill at Toranagallu in Karnataka, India (UNFCCC CDM Registration No. 0325), the power plant operators argued that they had to buy the waste gas generated by the steel mill at the same price per energy unit as coal, while it was actually free of charge. This made the power plant look financially unattractive. Power plant operators and the steel mill belonged to the same group of companies – so the loss made by the power plant operators due to the artificially high cost of the waste gas became the steel millers' gain. For a more detailed description of the case see Michaelowa (2007), and Mate and Ghosh (2009).

3.3.2 Prevention, Detection, and Enforcement

Independent private auditors have been required from the beginning to validate CDM documentation. At least in the first years of the CDM, these DOEs were unable to uncover cases of manipulation. CDM regulators realized this after the criticism of non-additional activities increased from 2007 onward (Michaelowa, 2007). After various suspensions of DOEs in late 2008 and early 2009 due to a lack of competence of their validation and verification personnel, insufficient evidence that they actually undertook independent technical reviews, and noncompliance with internal review or audit procedures to ensure sufficient quality (Schneider and Mohr, 2010: 5), the share of projects that were not validated significantly increased. This shows that independent audits can work if the regulators exercise sufficient oversight (Michaelowa and Buen, 2012). In their empirical assessment of downward manipulation of IRRs Chen and colleagues (2021) found that the problem has significantly decreased since 2008. Moreover, it is lower for DOEs affiliated to one of the big four accounting firms that face a higher risk of reputational damage. As discussed above, incentives for DOEs to report manipulation could be further increased if they were contracted by regulators rather than by activity developers.

The CDM Accreditation Panel (2008: 3) explicitly mentions "incidents of attempts of falsification of documents by project participants." To prevent such behavior, the UK CDM authority requires project developers to sign a declaration certifying that their information is correct and holds them criminally liable if fraud is discovered (Buen and Michaelowa, 2009). However, to date no legal case has been brought by the UK CDM authority against any CDM developer. Given that there is no evidence that the CDM projects approved by UK authorities were of better quality than average, the law seems to have been toothless.

Ex post checks of differences between projected and actual plant load factors by regulators can be a powerful tool to uncover additionality fraud. The CDM regulators' rejection of emission credits issuance for a hydro project in Brazil and a wind project in India due to plant load factor fraud (CDM Executive Board, 2011a, 2011b) sets an excellent precedent. In the future, minimum performance parameters, such as plant load factors for projects of certain types, should be defined for each host country based on good practice recommendations of local research institutions. Likewise, parameters used in the investment test should be vetted by a local expert.

Whenever transfer prices are used, the investment test should be done at the level of the full group of companies involved.

4 Cap-and-Trade Systems

Cap-and-trade markets are usually designed by a central authority, whose regulators choose between different design options when creating such markets. Central design decisions taken in the establishment of such systems, therefore, play a much greater role in creating risks or distortions to the efficiency and effectiveness of the market. By contrast, in baseline-and-credit systems project-specific rules are more important, and lobbying is more decentralized and focused on individual projects. To reflect this fundamental difference, this section approaches the issue from a different angle, focusing on design risks and the significant lobbying effort policymakers are exposed to in the process of passing cap-and-trade legislation (see Figure 4). The strategies of lobbyists differ depending on whether they are to be likely winners or losers of the system.

First, lobbyists – mainly from companies expected to be losers irrespective of the specific design – may try to prevent the enactment of the bill altogether. As shown by Meng and Rode (2019), lobbying lowered the probability of enacting the Waxman-Markey Bill by 13 percentage points because losing companies were able to lobby more effectively compared to winning ones. Interestingly,

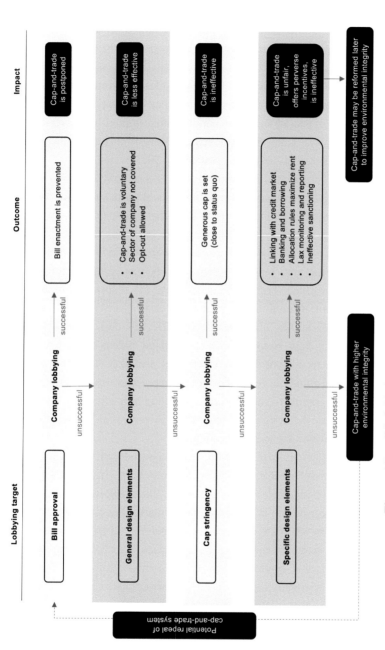

Figure 4 Possible lobbying efforts against cap-and-trade legislation

Source: Own graphic.

the potential winners under the bill spent more overall on lobbying but may have been less well organized or able to gather information.

Second, if the introduction of a cap-and-trade system as such cannot be prevented, companies will lobby either for a voluntary approach, for reduced coverage, or for opt-out options, which may allow them to be exempted from the legislation.

Third, if this strategy is unsuccessful and the system is introduced, they will lobby for more specific design options which may increase different risks, including the risks of overallocation, of ending with a surplus, or of overshooting the cap (see below). Thus, the first lobbying effort would be to end up with a generous cap close to the status quo (Grumbach, 2015).

Fourth, if there is no chance of preventing a cap-and-trade system from being introduced or of rendering it ineffective, lobbyists will try to keep costs as low as possible or even gain additional rents by targeting different design features. The design elements targeted in this way are those providing flexibility to the cap such as linking with credit markets or banking and borrowing possibilities; allocation rules which will maximize their rent such as grandparenting; lax monitoring, reporting, and verification rules, which may reduce the number of allowances to be surrendered; and low detection and penalty rates in case of noncompliance (Markussen and Svendsen, 2005; see also Wettestad and Jevnaker, 2016, on how Europe's energy-intensive industry decided they would not be able to prevent the introduction of a market stability reserve, and therefore decided to fight for other reform options that would compensate them for losses in competitiveness). Again, lobbying may affect the system's design in such a way that it may lead to perverse incentives and unfair allocations, or that it increases the risk of cheating.

Of course, the policy process is not linear. Once introduced, policies do not remain static, but may be reformed, replaced or repealed. This is particularly true in such a novel policy field as carbon markets. The example of the EU ETS shows that successive reform efforts can improve market design and overcome the past influence of lobbyists. Wettestad and Jevnaker (2016), for example, have analyzed the conditions that made the significant structural reforms to the EU ETS in 2015 possible, emphasizing the role of domestic political changes in key member states (Germany), of the EU ETS's embedding in a broader climate and energy package that allowed for more integrative bargaining and side-payments, and of more unified positions between member states and within the main EU institutions on the need for reform. On the other hand, the example of the failed Australian ETS in 2014 shows that the influence of industry can be so strong that a carbon market can be repealed if it is perceived to impose unacceptable costs on industry, even though it included significant compensation for the fossil fuel-dependent sectors (Pearse, 2016).

Figure 4 illustrates these potential impacts of lobbying efforts at the various ETS design steps. In the following sections, the different risks are assessed in more detail starting with the risk related to the cap followed by risks related to specific design features.

4.1 Risks Related to Cap Stringency

Overallocation happens ex ante, when more allowances are allocated than needed, such as in the form of hot air. A surplus may accumulate during the trading phase (e.g., due to unforeseen economic recessions, reductions resulting from overlapping policies such as subsidies for renewable energy, or a large supply of cheap offsets from linked systems) but can also be the result of initial overallocation.

In practice, a surplus or an overallocation in a cap-and-trade system result in the same situation, namely that the supply of allowances exceeds the demand.

4.1.1 Impact on Economic Efficiency and Environmental Integrity

Overallocation and surplus accumulation directly affect the effectiveness of a cap-and-trade system as they lead to a very low or even zero market price. This will question the introduction and effectiveness of the ETS as such as the incentive to actually reduce emissions will be low or nonexistent. Low prices may then lead regulators to intervene and lower the surplus. So far, most of the real-life cap-and-trade systems have suffered from overallocation (see examples below). In theory, there is also a risk of setting a too ambitious target with an overly stringent cap. This, in turn, would lead to a situation where carbon prices are very high and regulated entities are unable to comply, facing penalties as well as a negative impact on competitiveness. This may cause leakage, which would put politicians under pressure to adjust the cap. However, such situations have so far not been observed in reality.

Overall efficiency is affected by overallocation since it is likely that regulators have not been efficient in allocating the reductions for the economic sectors covered by the ETS and for those not covered by the ETS. In theory, the cap setting should take into account the cost of reducing emissions in each of those two groups. The group with higher costs would get a more generous allocation and the other a more stringent cap. If there is overallocation in one group, it is very likely that higher reductions are required in the other group which reduces efficiency.

In the case of a surplus, this would mean that the reduction costs were overestimated and/or the technical reduction potential underestimated, which may also result in an inefficient allocation between the two groups.

A certain surplus may be unproblematic as regulated companies may want to hedge against future price increases which could be backed by the surplus allowances. However, if the surplus volume of unused allowances increases beyond the hedging demand of participants (e.g., electricity utilities buying futures of allowances to reduce the carbon price risk for their sales of electricity), Neuhoff and colleagues (2012) argued that speculators may enter the market requiring high returns, which will result in highly discounted allowance prices relative to expected future prices. This could lead to inefficient investment decisions by market participants using the discounted price as reference for investment decisions.

4.1.2 Examples

The risk of overallocation can be explained using three examples from the international level:

First, experiences in the Kyoto Protocol's first commitment period from 2008 to 2012 show that due to the non-ratification of the Kyoto Protocol by the United States and the generous targets for most economies in transition, the international carbon market was overallocated from the outset. Although Annex I countries with Kyoto commitments had stated that they would refrain from buying hot air and implemented so-called Green Investment Schemes (GIS), the involvement of companies and the ability to buy ERUs from JI projects in countries in transition enabled imports of hot air into the Kyoto compliance market. This reduced the Protocol's environmental effectiveness since for each ERU laundering hot air, one additional tonne of GHG was emitted by the buyer (Kotsch et al., 2021).

Second, the overall inflow of hot air ERUs could have been manageable as the Kyoto Protocol limited the use of offsets by Annex I countries through its so-called supplementarity rule requiring that these mechanisms "be supplemental to domestic actions" (Art. 6.1 d, Art. 12.3 b, Art. 17), and stating that Kyoto units may only be used for compliance with *part* of Annex I countries' commitments. However, since no agreement on the quantitative implementation of supplementarity could be reached during the Kyoto Protocol negotiations, no limitation was imposed on the use of AAUs, CERs, and ERUs in the compliance assessment of the first commitment period.

The EU did specify a limit to be applied for member states when setting the cap for the ETS sector, and EU member states seem to use fewer ERUs or CERs compared to New Zealand, as can be seen in Figure 5. The extensive use of ERUs by New Zealand (NZ) can be explained by the fact that companies regulated by the NZETS were not bound by any quantitative restrictions on the use of CERs, ERUs, and RMUs for their compliance before May 31, 2015, when the surrendering of Kyoto units was stopped. Given the high volumes of Kyoto units being surrendered for compliance by NZ entities, the country was using those units for its own compliance. In any case, it seems that NZ put in less effort domestically and allowed a high share of Kyoto units with questionable quality to be bought from other countries, thus violating the originally foreseen supplementarity rule. However, as there was no strict implementation of this rule, this had no consequences (Figure 5).

Third, overallocation also occurred when countries which did not ratify the second commitment period (2013–2020) of the Kyoto Protocol (e.g., Japan and NZ) failed to directly cancel the remaining units in their Party and company accounts. This has led to a situation in which the demand for units from those countries has ceased but the supply of excess units still remains. The fear of lawsuits for redress and the lack of rules applicable when Parties withdraw from an agreement need to be addressed in future international carbon market regimes.

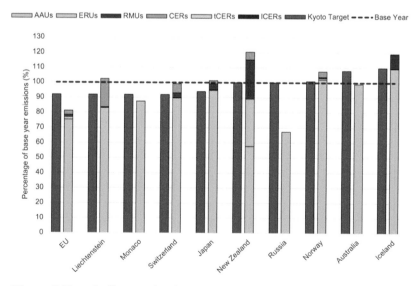

Figure 5 Use of offsets under the Kyoto Protocol's 1st Commitment Period

Source: Own graphic based on UNFCCC compliance data. The graph shows Annex I countries' Kyoto targets for the first commitment period and their use of the various types of Kyoto emission units for compliance.

Overallocation has also taken place in regional markets such as the EU ETS, as Figure 6 shows. For almost every year in the first 10 years since the system's introduction, the supply of allowances exceeded the demand. Only from 2014 onward, when part of the scheduled allocation was postponed to future years through so-called back-loading, the allocation stayed below the emissions. In Phases 1 and 2 of the EU ETS, the basis for cap setting were the National Allocation Plans (NAP) prepared by each member state and approved by the European Commission. This made it possible to lobby for generous allocation at the national level. Protectionist attitudes of some member states to set generous caps as well as the advantage of benefitting from financial transfers from member states with strict targets combined with a lax approval process of NAPs by the Commission in the first phase contributed to the overallocation (de Sepibus, 2007a).

In addition, Betz and Sato (2006) found that the enormous time pressure and some technical issues such as missing sector definitions, monitoring methodologies, and verification requirements combined with interpretation disputes with regard to coverage of certain processes created uncertainties in the data used to set the cap, which may also have contributed to the overallocation in the first phase of the EU ETS (2005–2007). Fortunately, this overallocation in the pilot phase was not bankable into the second phase (2008–2012). In the second phase, caps had to be in line with the Kyoto target of the respective member state. The Commission became stricter in assessing NAPs and did not accept cases where member states intended to assign the lion's share of the reduction effort to the non-ETS sectors (de Sepibus, 2007b). NAPs were also rejected if the caps were too generous, which was the case for almost all member states.

The second phase of the EU ETS illustrates how a surplus quickly builds up and is bankable into future periods. The unexpected financial crisis of 2008–2009 reduced emissions significantly (Bel and Joseph, 2015), which, combined with higher outcomes of complementary policies such as investments in renewables, resulted in annual surpluses that accumulated over time. But there were also design elements which increased the risk of a surplus. International credits increased the allowances supply by more than 1,500 million units, which is almost the size of the surplus. As ERUs and CERs were available at substantially lower prices than the EUA price, they were used extensively up to the limit and further reduced the EUA price (see Figure 6).

The possibility of banking units from Phase 2 into Phase 3 (2013-2020) led to a situation where the surplus also affected future periods. For example, from Phase 2 to Phase 3, 1,749.5 million allowances were banked (EC, 2015).

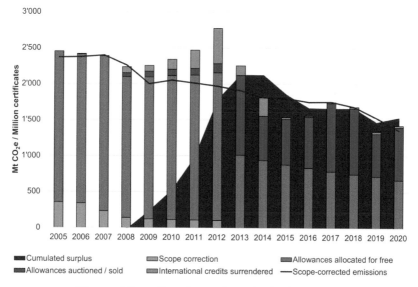

Figure 6 Overallocation and surplus in the EU ETS

Source: Own graphic based on data from the EEA EU ETS Dataviewer and from Commission communications on the total number of allowances in circulation and on international credit use in the EU ETS.[7] The cumulated surplus arises from the difference between all units used and the actual emissions.

The California ETS illustrates how overallocation can be the result of **overlapping policies**. In California, GHG reductions are mainly driven by Renewable Portfolio Standards to promote renewable energies as well as low-carbon fuel standards to promote investments into efficient combined-cycle gas plants. Borenstein and colleagues (2019) showed that for low reduction targets little additional abatement is needed, and therefore it is not surprising that the California Carbon Allowance prices cleared at or near the price floor and that the system is accumulating a surplus.

Linking with an overallocated system will **export the overallocation** to the other system. This experience can be illustrated by the link between the NZ ETS and the Kyoto mechanisms until 2015. The NZ ETS operated without a domestic cap and allowed an unlimited use of Kyoto units. With time, an oversupply of international Kyoto units such as CERs and ERUs accumulated. Their prices began to fall in 2011, which led to a decline in NZU prices (Figure 7). The sharp price decline reduced incentives for domestic reductions.

---

[7] https://ec.europa.eu/clima/news/updated-information-exchange-and-international-credits-use-eu-ets_en; https://ec.europa.eu/clima/sites/clima/files/ets/reform/docs/c_2021_3266_en.pdf; www.eea.europa.eu/data-and-maps/dashboards/emissions-trading-viewer-1.

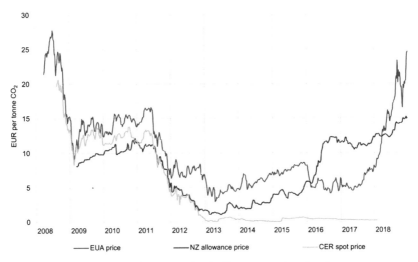

Figure 7 CER and New Zealand allowance price developments

Source: Own graphic based on data obtained from ICAP (EUA and NZ prices) and own data (CER prices). The curves show 7-day rolling averages of daily prices; CER prices are an average of Bluenext and ECX spot prices.

4.1.3 Prevention, Detection, and Enforcement

As the cap limits the tonnes of GHG emissions that can be released by the covered sectors over a certain period of time, setting the cap over a specified period at the "right" level is one of the critical decisions the regulator has to make to avoid overallocation from the outset. However, as shown in the above-mentioned examples, external factors and features such as complementary policies, flexibility through banking and borrowing, linking, and rules for using offsets or for the cancelling of units in case of withdrawal may alter the cap and have an impact on the risk of overallocation or surplus. To reduce the risk of overallocation it is important to implement **a solid cap setting process** and specify clear rules.

Since the cap will determine the price level, politicians and regulators in the cap setting process will be exposed to intensive lobbying and will, therefore, need to be politically assertive. Achieving the right balance of scarcity in the design process is challenging and will require solid information on, e.g., historic emissions, technology, and cost development, as well as an understanding of the quantitative impact of other design features and complementary policies affecting the scarcity of allowances. For decision-makers, it is not always easy to distinguish between truly relevant information and distorted information spread by special interest groups.

Setting the cap based on emission projections is particularly prone to result in overallocation. Such a counterfactual future development is highly uncertain as it depends on economic activity and technical innovation, as well as consumer behavior. In addition, there is a bias toward inflated projections because "no government likes to predict a gloomy economic future" (Grubb and Ferrario, 2006: 498). When the cutbacks are small relative to projections, the risk of ending up with overallocation is high. The quality of the forecast also depends on the reliability of historic data and accuracy in estimating the impact on emissions of complementary policies and measures.

Other solutions include cap-setting processes such as **intensity-based caps** or a flexible cap. Intensity-based caps allow the government to adjust the cap automatically to fluctuations in economic output. However, they will increase the risk that a certain emissions level is not met. They also come with some additional technical and administrative challenges and may lead to perverse incentives if they apply ex post allocation adjustments (see Section 4.3).

A **flexible cap** may be set in a way that it balances investor certainty with government flexibility by providing trajectories and corridors (see Figure 8). It allows for adjustment to unforeseen macro-economic developments, when new information in climate change science becomes available, when new GHG abatement technologies become available, or when the NDCs are adjusted in the process of increasing ambition.

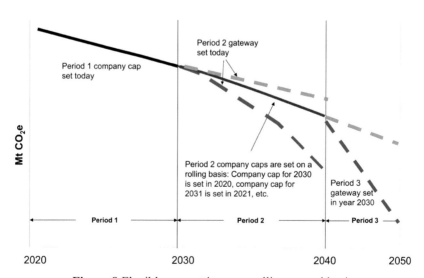

Figure 8 Flexible cap setting on a rolling annual basis

Source: Own graphic. Periods can vary, depending on the planning horizon of the industry covered. In this graph, 10 years are the length of a period. The gateway provides the upper and lower boundaries for the company cap.

The risk of accumulating a surplus can be reduced by **restrictive banking rules**, as in the first phase of the EU ETS (banking only within a phase and not between phases) or by limiting the number of allowances that entities can bank, as in the California ETS. However, this would come at a cost since the flexibility of banking reduces overall compliance costs and increases economic efficiency. In addition, it reduces price volatility as demonstrated above when the end of the first and second phases of the EU ETS were compared. At the end of the first phase, the price dropped to zero whereas banking from the second into the third trading period kept the price above zero because market participants expected future scarcity.

The risk of a surplus due to the inclusion of offsets may be reduced by **introducing a quantitative limit for offsets**. This also needs to be properly implemented and enforced to function well, as the experience with the "supplementarity" rule on the international level has illustrated.

Another way to reduce a surplus would be to **introduce a market stability mechanism** (see Wettestad and Jevnaker, 2016, 2019 for detailed discussions of the political processes that led to the introduction and later tightening of the EU ETS's market stability reserve). There are two types of control mechanisms: price-based or quantity-based. The former sets a maximum and/or minimum limit on the price of allowances, the latter a minimum and/or maximum abatement requirement within a given time period. Both can be used to adjust the supply of allowances in circulation by transferring them to a reserve. Such a supply adjustment can either be temporary, meaning the allowances in the reserve are released at a later stage, or permanent, meaning the cap is adjusted and allowances in the reserve are canceled. By cancelling allowances permanently, the environmental effectiveness of the ETS is increased. For the California ETS, Borenstein and colleagues (2019) showed that there is a very high likelihood that the price will be set by the price floor or the price cap. The probability that a price *between* the price floor and the price cap emerges is low because the marginal abatement cost curve in California is not responsive toward higher reductions. In such settings, greater attention should be put on setting the price floor and price cap compared to setting the emissions cap, which would favor hybrid price and quantity systems. If allowances are canceled from the reserve (as in the EU ETS) there is the potential risk of a self-fulfilling prophecy: Companies invest in mitigation measures anticipating higher carbon prices in the future as a result of the introduction of the reserve. This lowers the demand for allowances and thus leads to an increased transfer of surplus allowances to the reserve. After the permanent cancellation of the allowances, allowance prices rise as scarcity increases. Hence, while the market reserve works well for preventing price decreases associated with a surplus, it might lead to stronger price rises than without the mechanism.

4.2 Risk of Overshooting the Cap

Overshooting the cap refers to a situation in which the real aggregated emissions of the regulated entities are higher than the cap set or the allowances budget. Reasons for overshooting the cap include sanctions without make-good provisions, gaps in insolvency proceedings, lax verification rules, price caps, linking with weak systems, or non-permanence when including sinks since sequestered CO_2 may be released, for example, due to a fire. Some of those reasons are interrelated and may, as mentioned earlier, be the result of lobbying for weaker regulations.

Different reasons for overshooting the cap also incur different **sanctions** (Stranlund et al., 2011):

1) If a company surrenders fewer allowances than required according to its verified report, it receives a penalty for noncompliance.
2) If a company underreports its emissions, the difference between its actual emissions and the required allowances may not be immediately evident. However, if underreporting is detected, sanctions are imposed for violating the reporting requirements as well as for noncompliance.

The likelihood of overshooting the cap depends not only on the level but also on the type of penalty. In the case of a fixed penalty rate, meaning a constant fine for each missing allowance, overshooting is more likely to occur the closer the penalty level is to the market allowance price. As noncompliant companies pay the fine without having to surrender the missing allowances, the result will be higher emissions compared to the cap. Such a penalty would have a similar impact as a price cap (see Section 4.1.3).

If the penalty is implemented as a make-good provision, which requires companies to make up for their permit shortfalls according to a particular ratio (e.g., a 1:2 ratio will require two allowances to be surrendered in a future period for each permit shortfall), there may be a temporary overshooting as companies are allowed to borrow allowances from future periods. The make-good cannot continue indefinitely but is usually restricted to a certain period before companies lose their operation license. Unlike the fixed penalty rate, the maximum cost of compliance under the make-good-provision is reliant on future allowance prices. Thus, greater uncertainty about future allowance prices will increase the likelihood of compliance as the level of the penalty will probably be high.

Finally, a combination of the two penalty types, a so-called mixed penalty, can apply. This would mean that there is a financial penalty, but, in addition, the missing allowances must be surrendered in the future. Thus, the overshooting risk is mainly related to fixed financial penalty rates without make-good provisions.

In case of an **insolvency proceeding**, it is often unclear who must surrender the allowance, which may also lead to overshooting the cap. The insolvent company may, for example, have sold emission allowances that it was allocated free of charge, and, therefore, it may no longer hold any allowances at the time of surrendering them. If such situations are not explicitly regulated by making the insolvency administrator be the one to surrender the missing allowances on behalf the insolvent company, overshooting of the cap may occur (Schumacher, 2020).

Emissions trading systems which have established a **price cap** will also overshoot the emission cap if the price cap is triggered and additional allowances are issued.

Linking with another cap-and-trade system will import all the risks of that other system – or even of the systems linked to it. This includes the risk of overshooting the cap, for example, in case weaker sanctions are applied in the linked systems. In addition, linking will also result in risks related to the loss of control over the design, operation, and enforcement (Green et al., 2014; Haites, 2016). For example, a lower monitoring, reporting, and verification (MRV) standard or lax enforcement in the other system may reduce the effectiveness of both systems as it may increase emissions and lower prices compared to the situation before linking. In practice, however, linking of carbon markets has been much more elusive than expected, in part due to insufficient compatibility between their designs (Gulbrandsen et al., 2019).

Overshooting the cap will be more likely when GHG with more complex MRV or if **biological sinks** such as forests are included in the system. Forests bear the risk of releasing sequestered carbon due to storms, floods, fires, or deforestation. Forests also require different MRV standards and entail greater uncertainty due to more complex natural processes. In this context, the question also arises as to the definition of "forest."[8]

Overshooting of the cap will happen if the **obligation to surrender** allowances does not correspond to a one-for-one system but follows a progressive system under which one allowance is surrendered for two tonnes of CO_2.

---

[8] In addition, the inclusion of forests may lead to higher emissions outside of the cap as the risk of leakage has to be taken into account. This means it must be ensured that afforestation in one region will not result in deforestation in an unregulated region.

4.2.1 Impact on Efficiency and Environmental Integrity

Overshooting the cap will mainly impact environmental integrity of the system as there will be more emissions than originally foreseen. As there will be less demand for allowances, the price of allowances will fall. There may be a trade-off between efficiency and environmental integrity to be made as overshooting the cap may be more likely when more sources are covered and systems are linked. At the same time, a broader coverage, such as including more diverse emission sources, usually increases efficiency since the more heterogeneous the installations that are covered, the greater the cost dispersion of the available reduction options will be. This will result in higher efficiency gains due to trading.

4.2.2 Examples

Most ETS systems apply a mixed **penalty** system and thus require make-good provisions, so that real cases of overshooting the cap are not known. Only the Korean ETS applies a financial penalty only.

Insolvencies have increased in recent years since the coronavirus pandemic has hit the economy. The current legislation, for example in Germany, does not yet address this issue properly and it is unclear what will happen if companies do not surrender enough allowances when becoming insolvent.

Linking of emissions trading systems has so far been implemented only when the regulations are almost identical. For example, the link between the EU and Swiss ETS required the Swiss ETS to adopt similar penalty levels including a make-good provision.

The NZ ETS linked with the international Kyoto market and, in addition, had a **fixed price** at which unlimited number of NZ units were issued. The so-called **progressive surrendering** obligation under the NZ ETS, under which one unit was surrendered for two tonnes of emissions (either Kyoto or NZ issued units) was introduced in 2009 and was phased out stepwise until January 2019. This approach clearly makes it more challenging to meet a cap and bears the risk of overshooting it if it is not properly managed (Leining et al., 2020).

In most ETS systems, **coverage** of GHG has been restricted to simple-to-monitor gases such as CO_2. Sinks have only been included directly in the NZ ETS, or indirectly – via offsets – in the California ETS. Sources that are more complex to quantify, such as N_2O emissions from fertilizers, have been included on an upstream (e.g., the retailer selling the fertilizer) rather than a downstream level (e.g., the farm using the fertilizer), which makes rigorous reporting and verification easier. However, on the international carbon market, which is based on national inventories and AAU trading, underreporting of fluorocarbons has been detected. For example, the Swiss research institute Empa discovered that Italian installations emit 10 to 20 times more HFC-23 than reported in official UNFCCC inventories.[9]

4.2.3 Prevention, Detection, and Enforcement

As explained above, a high financial penalty combined with a make-good provision is the best way to reduce the risk of overshooting the cap. The financial penalty acts as a deterrent, and in case of noncompliance the missing allowances will be surrendered the year after. An option for systems without a make-good provision would be for the government to use the penalty payment to buy the missing allowances, canceling them after purchase. In case of insolvency, legislation needs to be in place to ensure that the insolvency administrator fulfils the duty to surrender the required allowances and in case of noncompliance complies with the make-good provision (Schumacher, 2020).

The risk of linking with other systems may be reduced by requiring similar standards in cap setting, MRV, or sanctions, as provided for in the linking agreement between the EU and the Swiss ETS.[10] However, this is not enough: A joint oversight system is also necessary to address issues related to international fraud (see Section 5.4).

The non-permanence risk in sequestration projects may be addressed in different ways: First, in case of reversals the emissions could be required to be compensated for by allowances, as it is done in the New Zealand system for forestry.[11] Second, insurance could be required for offsets from forestry projects. Third, a buffer pool[12] could be introduced to address potential reversals. Finally, under the CDM the risk was addressed by issuing only temporary credits, which had to be replaced or renewed. These different approaches may be combined.

The risk of CO_2 leakage may be addressed by covering all land areas within a jurisdiction and applying satellite data to detect leakages.

Satellite data has been used to measure national HFC emissions and reveal discrepancies to the reported values. For example, in the case of HFC-134a, emissions were found to be 79 percent lower compared to official UNFCCC inventory totals, while other HFC emissions were significantly greater than the reported values (Lunt et al., 2015). Applying satellite data may therefore be

---

[9] www.empa.ch/de/web/s604/schummelei-in-der-statistik.
[10] See www.fedlex.admin.ch/eli/cc/2018/124/de.
[11] www.mpi.govt.nz/dmsdocument/6991-An-Overview-of-Forestry-in-the-ETS.
[12] In a buffer solution, not all certificates from a sink project portfolio are issued, but a certain percentage of all certificates ends up in a buffer. If there is a "reversal" of the sink, certificates from the buffer are used to compensate for the resulting CO_2 emissions.

a way to include other GHG in ETS systems and verify the quality of reporting (see also Section 5.1) to reduce the risk of overshooting the cap.

4.3 Risk of Creating Perverse Incentives

The allocation process is particularly prone to lobbying efforts as it has distributional effects and creates winners or losers. There is, therefore, a high risk that the implemented rules serve to maximize the rent rather than being fair or efficient. There are two options: Either allowances are allocated for free to regulated entities or other beneficiaries, which means these will receive the respective value, or they are auctioned and the authority receives the value as auction revenue. The latter would be in line with the polluter-pays principle and has the advantage that it treats incumbents and newcomers equally. Therefore, auctioning should be the favored option (Hepburn et al., 2006). However, free allocation is politically easier to implement because companies bear only the cost of the abatement but not of their emissions, meaning they have more money to invest in abatement opportunities. In addition, incumbents like the fact that it may create barriers for new market entrants (Hepburn et al., 2006). One of the many negative effects of free allocation is the fact that companies might not realize that the freely allocated allowances have a value (the so-called opportunity cost) because they can be sold at a price on the market.

There are two major methods of free allocation, but many other combinations are possible: Grandparenting is based on a company's historical emissions, whereas benchmarking uses a rate based on the most efficient installations or technologies within a regulated industry. Both methods may create perverse incentives for emission abatement if provisions allow for the updating of the allocation based on changes to production activity or plant capacity (Sartor et al., 2014; Verde et al., 2018). Further, if under benchmarking with updating based on output, the companies are not aware of the opportunity cost of holding the allowances, they may not realize cheap reduction options that would allow them to sell allowances with a net benefit. This is not efficient, as it causes market participants to forgo trades that would be more advantageous.

As allocation is often used to compensate for the additional cost of reducing emissions or buying allowances or to help ensure competitiveness between domestic and foreign companies, there is a clear trade-off between efficiency and competitiveness. The use of income from penalty payments can also create perverse incentives, especially for state-owned companies.

4.3.1 Impact on Efficiency and Environmental Integrity

From an economic point of view, the environmental integrity of a system is not affected by the allocation method as long as the cap remains unaltered. However, as explained above, free allocation may reduce the incentive to abate, therefore shifting the abatement requirement to other sectors or to installations without free allocation, which has a negative impact on efficiency.

In contrast to traditional economic theory, efficiency seems to also be affected when the allocation of an individual plant is higher or lower than its emissions (long or short companies). Research has shown that net buyers (i.e., companies that do not have enough initial allowances to cover their emissions) tend to be more active in the carbon market than net sellers (Cludius and Betz, 2020; Abrell et al., 2021): Those companies with more emissions than their free allocation are likely to become active to avoid a penalty for noncompliance (which in the EU ETS is higher than the market price) and, in addition, to avoid having to make good for the missing allowances. Net sellers may hoard allowances instead of selling them because they will not face such pressure. When they do not become active in the market, the allowance price increases because fewer allowances are available, which reduces efficiency (Burtraw and McCormack, 2016).

Finally, if free allocation also includes updating, this may create a perverse incentive to increase emissions or output in order to increase the reference level for future free allocation. Once again, the allowance price will not reflect the true reduction cost, which will affect efficiency (Neuhoff et al., 2015). Auctioning, on the other hand, will force market participants to reveal their willingness to pay for allowances, making the auction price efficient.

4.3.2 Examples

Lobbying Effort and Rent Seeking in the EU ETS

There is evidence that substantial lobbying took place in the early years of the EU ETS to increase the rent from primary allocation. As explained above, in the first two phases the EU member states were responsible for developing NAPs, which had to be approved by the EU Commission (Bailey and Maresh, 2009). Cludius (2018) and Morris (2012) assessed which companies had the largest surplus of free allocation in Phase 1 and Phase 2, respectively. Both studies show that it was especially companies in the steel and cement sectors that had excess allocations and that the level of excess allocation was a major determinant for which companies would become potential "winners" or "losers." There is anecdotal evidence to support the claim that ArcelorMittal, one of the world's leading steel producers, had a particularly sophisticated lobbying strategy. In Luxembourg, for example, the allocation formula for the NAP 2005–2007 included a projection factor aimed to account for the change in capacity utilization due to the economic conditions in 2005–2007. ArcelorMittal had agreed with the Luxemburg government to enter into the formula an annual growth forecast value of 4 percent, although other studies projected a growth of only 1.6 percent. This reduced the company's need for buying or shifting surplus allowances from other sites and increased their income from selling surplus allowances. Further reports on lobbying affecting the design of the EU ETS can be found in Jevnaker and Wettestad (2017) and Wettestad and Jevnaker (2016, 2019).

Lobbying for Windfall Profits

Windfall profits are another example of successful lobbying. Companies can generate a profit by passing on the opportunity costs to consumers through higher prices even though the allowances have been allocated free of charge. With grandparenting, companies may decrease their output in order minimize their liability, which leads to an increase in product prices. With higher product prices, profits increase and may prolong the lifetime of high-carbon assets and result in higher costs of emission reductions compared to a situation where allowances were auctioned. In Phases 1 and 2, the large share of free allocation led to a high level of windfall profits for electricity producers and other industry sectors. As described above, they were able to pass on the nominal costs of allowances – which they had received for free – to their consumers. According to empirical and model findings, for example, CO_2 cost pass-through rates varied between 60 and 100 percent for wholesale power markets in Germany and the Netherlands in 2005–2006 (Sijm et al., 2006). This led to significant wealth transfers from consumers to producers, estimated to be around EUR 13 billion per year for Phase 1 (Keppler and Cruciani, 2010).

Perverse Incentives and Distortions due to Allocation Rules

Intensity-based climate targets: In the Chinese pilot systems of Shenzhen and Hubei, intensity-based climate targets were used to reduce the risk of under- or over-supply. To some extent, this mechanism subsidized additional emissions, leading to low marginal abatement requirements while reducing allocation when efficiency is improved, thus reducing the incentive for low-carbon investment (Zhang et al., 2021).

Updating between phases: In around 10 EU member states, the allocation received in Phase 2 was a function of emissions in 2005, which provided a perverse incentive for less abatement in 2005 in order to receive more permits in Phase 2 (Neuhoff et al., 2006).

Early action: If grandparenting is used for allocation, there are no incentives for companies to invest in emission reductions as this would reduce the amount they will be allocated. At the international level, if Article 6 rules under the Paris Agreement specify that only activities outside the scope of NDCs can be traded internationally to avoid double-counting, there is a perverse incentive to keep the scope of the NDC narrow in order to sell more units internationally.

New entrant and closure rules: If new entrants do not receive free allocations, and this coincides with the withdrawal of allocations to "ceasing installations," efficiency is affected since this creates perverse incentives to keep inefficient plants in operation. Companies wishing to enter a sector may be at a disadvantage because they do not receive free allocation. The reduced competition from this barrier to entry will delay decisions on emission reductions for incumbents, which choose instead to increase emissions since they are able to absorb the additional increase in costs. The barrier to entry may also prevent companies with new, low-emission technologies from entering the market. In addition, free allocation to new entrants based on benchmarks on installed capacity, as done in Phase 1 and 2 of the EU ETS by several member states, leads to perverse incentives to build oversized new installations such as boilers (as was experienced in Denmark).

Output-based allocation: In the EU ETS, allowances are allocated based on benchmarks multiplied by output for installations in sectors classified as at risk of leakage, the output being updated regularly. Output-based allocation reduces the marginal cost of production compared to other allocation mechanisms (which acts like an indirect subsidy) and will lead to imperfect pass-through of allowance costs to consumers. This undermines the incentive for consumers to change their behavior by consuming fewer emissions-intensive products or choosing less emissions-intensive alternatives. This form of allocation is used to reduce the risk of carbon leakage which happens when either production or productive capacity is transferred outside of the area of the cap-and-trade system. Because the transfer reduces emissions in the jurisdiction under the ETS while increasing emissions outside of it, there is no decrease in emissions at the global level (Neuhoff et al., 2015).

Technology-specific benchmarks: If technology-specific benchmarks are applied to the power sector, as in the Korean and Chinese cap-and-trade systems, incentives for low-carbon investments will be reduced because the benchmarks that apply to lower-carbon generation sources are usually more stringent. This creates a perverse incentive to keep, rather than replace, emissions-intensive generators (Acworth and Kuneman, forthcoming).

Ex post allocation adjustments: The Mexican pilot cap-and-trade system provides for an ex post allocation adjustment, which can alter the allowance supply if it is not strictly applied in accordance with pre-set cap levels. In addition, it lowers the incentive to reduce output (Acworth and Kuneman, forthcoming).

Compensation for Increased Electricity Costs

In the EU ETS, the incentive to invest in energy-efficiency improvements has also been dampened because of compensation given to energy-intensive firms considered to be at risk of carbon leakage. Where companies do not care about electricity costs because of the compensation they receive, emissions and allowance prices will remain higher than what would be optimal. In countries (e.g., Germany) where this compensation is clearly phased out over time and where benchmarks based on recent data are used to calculate compensation levels, such distortions are reduced. However, electricity price compensation also plays an important role in reducing leakage risk. Therefore, there is a trade-off between leakage protection and losses in efficiency.

A similar rule applies in the Korean ETS, where producers receive compensation for net allowance costs, which provides an incentive to invest in more expensive reduction options and thus increases the allowance price (Acworth and Kuneman, forthcoming).

Perverse Incentive Related to Noncompliance

This example is based on a white certificate system in New South Wales (NSW), Australia, although this type of perverse incentive and governance failure may also occur in a carbon ETS. First, it is important to note that the revenue from penalty payments is absorbed into NSW's general government budget.

The noncompliance rate of certain retailers was surprisingly high, with penalty payments peaking in 2010 at around AUD 7 million; interestingly, the retailers with the highest shortfall were both owned by the NSW government. In addition, the rules of the system allowed retailers to pass on the penalty to electricity consumers. Rather than investing in energy efficiency, government-owned retailers seem to have been happy to pay a penalty which not only increased the NSW general budget but was in fact passed on to consumers (Betz et al., 2013).

4.3.3 Prevention, Detection, and Enforcement

One solution to prevent many of the above-mentioned perverse incentives would be to replace free allocation by auctioning, such as in the RGGI in the United States. If full auctioning is implemented, companies will not lobby for specific allocation favors, nor will windfall profits occur.

To prevent distortions from compensation mechanisms, they must be abolished. Instead, a border adjustment mechanism may be required to reduce the risk of leakage.

The risk of perverse incentives for state-owned companies could be eliminated by earmarking the revenue from penalty payments for reduction measures. For example, instead of being fed into the government's general budget, the penalty payments could go into a separate account, such as a climate technology fund.

5 Cross-Cutting Risks

In addition to the risks associated with either baseline-and-credit mechanisms or cap-and-trade systems, there are also risks which apply to both types of market mechanism. These are explained in the following sections.

5.1 Monitoring, Reporting, and Verification Risks

MRV (i.e., monitoring, reporting, and verification) refers to the rules and processes that need to be in place to ensure the transparent and accurate tracking of emissions and emission reductions within the scope of a carbon market. They include the regular monitoring of the emissions at each regulated installation based on an approved monitoring plan and methodology, the submission of emissions reports, and the verification of these reports by an independent auditor.

Monitoring: First, it must be established which sources of emissions are to be monitored, including by setting a minimum size threshold for covered sources. This is usually done in a monitoring plan. As a recent case involving a chemical plant in Switzerland shows, an emission source can easily be omitted.[13] Second, the plan needs to include a monitoring method, such as continuous measurement and/or calculation of emissions. The method chosen will determine the reporting frequency and the verification requirements. Calculation methods are usually differentiated by tiers, where higher quality and accuracy requirements apply to larger sources and lower requirements to smaller ones (PMR and ICAP, 2021). However, there can be a trade-off between a very accurate method and the potential for abusing this methodology. For example, standardized emissions factors are not very accurate, but they are easier to verify and provide relatively limited opportunity for cheating. In contrast, if the carbon content of fuels is determined on site, which is more accurate, the sampling method can be manipulated to yield more favorable outcomes. There are anecdotal reports from the early years of the EU ETS of such samples being taken only from coal piles with a low carbon content. This is why the EU ETS now requires a sampling plan.

---

[13] www.parlament.ch/de/ratsbetrieb/suche-curia-vista/geschaeft?AffairId=20203045.

Reporting: Many ETSs rely on self-monitoring and self-reporting. However, to ensure the quality of the reported information, an inspection of the data is often required. Electronic systems have been established to handle the reporting and allow for easy comparison and statistical analysis (ECA, 2015). However, in the EU ETS the member states implemented their MRV systems at different jurisdictional levels. Some involve regional and/or local authorities, and there are also differences in how reporting is enforced (ECA, 2015).

Verification: Verification is often outsourced to private auditors or verifiers, which raises the question as to their trustworthiness. As a result, there is often a need to inspect the verifiers or to establish an accreditation body. In many ETSs, companies can select their own verifier. Given that verification is a recurring service to those companies, there is a conflict of interest for verifiers (see also Section 3.1). In the EU ETS, there is a lack of standards for documenting verification findings, and processes are missing on how to resolve identified problems. The probability of spot-checks by the regulator has also not been harmonized among EU member states.

5.1.1 Impact on Efficiency and Environmental Integrity

Lax MRV rules will directly affect the environmental integrity of an ETS because they generate an incentive to decrease emissions to a lesser extent than required (in the expectation that the shortfall will not be detected). Actual GHG in the atmosphere will then increase more than is reported. In addition, lax MRV rules will affect the efficiency of the market since underreporting resulting from less rigorous MRV rules will reduce the demand for allowances from regulated companies. This, in turn, will lead to a lower allowance price compared to a situation with correct reporting. The incentive to underreport emissions is particularly high when allowance prices are high (McAllister, 2010) because companies will compare the opportunity costs of buying additional allowances with the probability of being detected and the penalty they will have to pay for underreporting and noncompliance.

5.1.2 Examples

If MRV rules are lax, there is a risk that a reported tonne of CO_2e does not equal a real tonne – for example, if the report is based on erroneous data. To guarantee trust in the carbon market and ensure that allowances can be traded as a fungible – i.e., interchangeable – commodity, a reliable MRV system is crucial. As the experience with the EU ETS has shown (Betz, 2016; EC, 2021), MRV should be started as early as possible as it takes time for companies to establish the process and procure the equipment needed.

5.1.3 Prevention, Detection, and Enforcement

Generally, the probability of a violation being detected and the penalty for noncompliance are the key parameters to ensure both compliance and correct reporting. However, increasing the probability of detection (e.g., through a higher number of on-the-spot inspections) also increases administrative costs. This suggests that, theoretically, the best approach should involve only a minimum number of inspections but a high penalty for noncompliance.

Many ETSs have implemented a two-layered monitoring system in which the company self-reports emissions, an independent verifier checks the report, and an authority spot-checks the verifier. As the example of the New South Wales GGAS shows, and as mentioned in Section 3 with regard to the role of verifiers in baseline-and-credit systems, truthful reporting depends on the impartiality of the verifiers and on incentivizing them to detect violations (Shen et al., 2020).

5.2 Risk of Double Counting

Schneider and colleagues (2019: 180) defined double counting as "counting the same emission reduction [or removal] more than once to achieve climate mitigation targets." Failure to prevent double counting results in greater GHG emissions than those reported by participants in the carbon market. For this reason, avoiding double counting is key to ensuring the **environmental integrity** of carbon markets at all levels. At the same time, avoiding double counting is necessary to maintain the **trust of market participants** concerning the value of the units they are acquiring.

Double counting can occur both in baseline-and-credit and cap-and-trade systems and at different stages of the market cycle:

– **Double issuance** occurs when "more than one unit [allowance or credit] is issued for the same emission or emission reduction" (Schneider et al., 2015: 474). Double issuance is most likely when there is a fragmented carbon market. If there are two or more systems whose registries are not connected, it is possible that they issue units for the same reduction.
– **Double claiming** happens when "the same emission reduction is counted twice towards attaining mitigation pledges," for example toward a country's own climate pledge while being sold as an offset in the international carbon market (Schneider et al., 2015: 475). Double claiming can also happen indirectly, for example, when a country pledges to reduce deforestation while at the same time selling credits from an efficient cookstove project (whose effect is also to reduce deforestation). Another potential source of double claiming are differences in accounting for indirect emissions, such as

from electricity consumption. Baseline-and-credit systems tend to award reduction credits to those entities that undertake the emission reductions, for example through energy efficiency measures, even though the actual reduction takes place upstream during electricity generation. Double counting occurs if the reductions are counted both downstream by issuing credits and upstream by reducing the number of allowances to be surrendered.

– **Double use** means that the same allowance or credit is used more than once to attain a mitigation pledge, in either the same or different countries (Schneider et al., 2015: 475). This may happen when a unit is transferred to another registry without being canceled in the original one, for example, when two ETSs are linked.

A final type of double counting occurs when emission reduction projects are used both within a carbon market and as part of climate finance provided to support developing country mitigation efforts (see, e.g., Michaelowa et al., 2020b).

5.2.1 Examples

Given that, so far, there have been few linkages between existing carbon markets, real-life examples of double counting are still rare.

One case mentioned in the literature pertains to the double use of CERs from CDM projects in 2009 and 2010, which was possible due to loopholes in the EU ETS market that have since been addressed (INTERPOL, 2013). In this case, Hungarian businesses had surrendered 2 million CERs to the government to compensate for their emissions. Anticipating that it would overachieve its Kyoto Protocol target, the Hungarian government decided to re-sell them, which it was allowed to do. What was not allowed was their re-use within the EU. Specifically, credits were sold to a Hungarian company, re-sold to a British trading company, and from there to a company in Hong Kong, which offered them for sale on a European carbon exchange. The final buyers were unaware that the credits had already been used in Europe. Once the carbon exchange discovered this, it suspended trading, managing to isolate the recycled credits and facilitating their buy-back (INTERPOL, 2013).

Instances of double counting are expected to increase in the future. The issue is being discussed in the context of Article 6 of the Paris Agreement (see Section 6.2), but it may also happen within other carbon markets. For example, double counting is possible in the context of the International Civil Aviation Organization (ICAO) Carbon Offsetting and Reduction Scheme for International Aviation (CORSIA) if a host country of an offsetting project used within CORSIA also counts those reductions toward its own NDC target (Schneider et al., 2019).

5.2.2 Prevention, Detection, and Enforcement

The examples of CORSIA and the CDM above highlight the fact that to avoid double counting, governance arrangements between authorities at various levels of governance or in different jurisdictions should be compatible. Such compatibility can be achieved through **policy coordination** – in the case of the Paris Agreement and ICAO, neither can "impose" its rules on the other; their respective parties need to agree on compatible rules among themselves. Compatibility can also be achieved through **policy emulation**, where one authority decides to adopt the solution implemented by the other authority.

The CDM example also emphasizes the importance of robust monitoring of unit transfers across exchanges in different jurisdictions and under different carbon market rules. Given that carbon market units are intangible assets, their traceability along the market chain is more difficult than that of physical commodities. Stricter and more consistent regulatory oversight across jurisdictions with compatible registries and transaction logs is, therefore, critically important to avoid double counting (INTERPOL, 2013; Schneider and La Hoz Theuer, 2019).

Within the carbon markets envisaged under the Paris Agreement, the solution proposed to avoid double claiming are so-called corresponding adjustments: Whenever a unit is transferred to a different country or system, it needs to be deducted from the transferring country's own NDC target, which, therefore, becomes more ambitious.

While the idea of corresponding adjustments is generally accepted in the post-Paris negotiations, it is still contested whether they should apply to emission reductions that fall outside the scope of countries' NDCs (e.g., in the case of developing countries with NDCs without economy-wide coverage), and whether they should also apply to the market mechanism planned under Article 6.4. If reductions outside the scope of NDCs are not counted, this may generate a perverse incentive to establish lax or narrower NDCs so that more units can be sold internationally (Schneider and La Hoz Theuer, 2019).

For these reasons, corresponding adjustments should be applicable to all transfers under the Paris Agreement, either within or outside the scope of NDCs, and either to countries or to other entities such as CORSIA. In addition, they should be applicable to all mechanisms. Finally, common GHG emission metrics should be applicable across all these systems. A country with an NDC target that is not expressed in terms of GHG emissions, would, therefore, have to translate it into the common metric before being allowed to participate in the carbon market (Schneider et al., 2019).

Past European regulations for avoiding double counting of ERUs from JI projects under the Kyoto Protocol and EUAs within the EU ETS introduced a form of corresponding adjustment that can inform the design of the market mechanisms under the Paris Agreement (Kollmuss et al., 2015).

5.3 Risk of Market Manipulation

Market manipulation is a form of market abuse in which market participants influence the market developments for personal gain, causing the price of allowances or credits to inflate or deflate artificially. This can be achieved through manipulative market behavior such as false or misleading transactions, price positioning, or the spread of false information. Manipulation can arise when individual market participants exploit information asymmetries even within an otherwise competitive market or by exercising market power. A dominant company which holds a significantly larger market share than its competitors has the power to restrict (extend) market output resulting in prices above (below) the efficient level, therefore generating positive real wealth without risk (Jarrow, 1992). Since companies participating in carbon markets typically belong to sectors with imperfect competition (e.g., the electricity sector), the exercising of market power in carbon markets represents a significant risk (Hintermann, 2016).

5.3.1 Initial Allocation of Allowances

Whether or not market manipulation through the exercise of market power occurs depends on the initial allocation of allowances. Under perfect competition, all companies in the carbon market are price-takers, and the carbon price equals the marginal abatement costs across all of them, regardless of the allocation mechanism (Hahn and Stavins, 2011). This is different in a market with imperfect competition: If the dominant company is a net seller of emissions allowances, it will set the price above the marginal abatement cost, increasing the demand by abating less than under perfect competition. In contrast, if the dominant company is a net buyer, it will try to decrease the allowance price and over-abate relative to the competitive abatement level (Liski and Montero, 2011; Hintermann, 2017). The effect on the market price is much stronger if the dominant company is a net seller because the ability of the net buyer company to manipulate the price downward is limited by its constraint to fulfil its compliance obligation (Hintermann, 2016). The overall amount of emission reductions is not affected in either of these cases (assuming functioning MRV), but efficiency is reduced because the equilibrium price does not correspond to the marginal abatement cost.

The solution to achieving an efficient outcome in a market with imperfect competition has long been to allocate to the dominant company exactly the number of allowances it needs to comply with regulations (Hahn, 1984). However, free and full allocation to the dominant company does not lead to an efficient outcome when taking into account the interactions between different markets (Sartzetakis, 1997; Liski and Montero, 2011; Hintermann, 2017). Market manipulation has an impact on both companies' compliance costs in the carbon market (through their purchases of allowances) and companies' revenues in the product market (by passing on the carbon price to consumers by means of increased product prices). In other words, manipulating the carbon market to achieve an inflated allowance price leads to an increase in compliance costs but will also increase the revenue in the product market. If the increased revenue in the product market outweighs the increased compliance costs, a dominant company with market power in the allowance market or in both markets has the incentive to manipulate the allowance price to maximize its profits in both markets. Considering both markets in the minimization of compliance costs will lead to a different expected behavior of the dominant company. If we consider that the net buyer minimizes its compliance cost in the allowance market only, the net buyer will always have an incentive to use market power to decrease the allowance price. In contrast, when profits are maximized in both markets and free allocation and cost pass-through prevail, the dominant net buyer may actually have an incentive to manipulate the price to create an upward trend (Hintermann, 2016).

5.3.2 Examples

While there are many economic theoretical studies and a few laboratory experiments on the existence of market manipulation in carbon markets, real-life evidence of market manipulation is scarce. Some studies have shown that companies were allocated more free allowances than needed in Phase 1 of the EU ETS, which led to positive correlation of allowance price and stock market returns and might have created an incentive to manipulate the price upward to maximize profits. However, no evidence of market power or attempted market manipulation has been presented (Oberndorfer, 2009; Hintermann, 2017). In California's regional Clean Air Incentive Market, 350,000 allowances worth USD 2.5 million expired unused. This suggests that manipulative activity could have been possible if costs had been passed on to consumers (Holland and Moore, 2012; Hintermann, 2016).

5.3.3 Impact on Efficiency and Environmental Integrity

Market manipulation leads to a situation where the market price does not reflect the marginal abatement costs and, therefore, the cheapest abatement options are not exhausted. This creates inefficiency and welfare loss as the societal costs to achieve a given emissions cap are larger compared to a situation without market manipulation. In the end, consumers and taxpayers suffer the consequences. Under free allocation with cost pass-through, even small price-taking companies benefit from increased allowance prices when a dominant company manipulates the market and will, therefore, not collude against the monopolistic firm.

Market manipulation can also have a negative impact on the environmental integrity of the market as with increasing mitigation costs the political willingness and enforceability of a stringent cap will be diminished (Hintermann, 2016).

5.3.4 Prevention, Detection, and Enforcement

While full and free allocation is not a solution to mitigate market power, it is unclear whether a double-auction format can prevent market manipulation.

Market manipulation in carbon markets is difficult to detect since data on abatement costs, allowance sales, and purchases are not readily available. In carbon markets where physical transaction records are available, such as in the EU ETS, information is available only on part of the market, namely the spot transactions where the allowance is directly transferred from seller to buyer. The other part of the market, which may be substantial in volume, is related to derivatives such as forwards and futures. These are not exchanged directly. Rather, the product value is determined by the underlying emission allowance. Futures contracts represent the obligation to trade an allowance at a set price in the future. Such data is fully transparent only to derivative exchanges or OTC service providers, but not to the regulators managing the ETS registry. The many markets and products make it difficult to detect manipulation and distinguish hedging strategies from abusive behavior. Increasing transparency by requiring the sharing derivative and OTC trading data with regulators (as in electricity markets) might make market manipulation easier to detect.

ETSs are especially prone to market manipulation at their beginning, when, to achieve political support for the market, the extent of free allocation might be large. As the EU ETS has shown, only a few, mainly large, companies enter the market in the beginning; this leads to a "thin" market prone to sharp price changes. For example, on July 14, 2005, at a time when the market was largely dominated by the French exchange – which was shut because of a national holiday – just a few OTC trades were able to decrease the price substantially.

This shows that the risks of market power abuse and collusion are even larger in markets with few participants and a large share of free allocation (Hintermann, 2016). In addition, the risk of market manipulation is larger in the first phase of a newly established ETS due to regulatory loopholes or the need for further harmonization to make it effective.

To reduce such risks, it is important to classify the legal and fiscal nature of an allowance from the beginning. It must be determined, for instance, whether allowances are considered as commodities or financial instruments under the law. This has implications for the legal regime in which they are regulated. More stringent regulation, with carefully defined conditions for market access, trading, and other market activities, can reduce the likelihood of market manipulation and improve transparency and accountability. At the same time, it entails higher administrative and transaction costs, and it can stifle market activity and reduce liquidity. A balance needs to be struck for each relevant context between under- and overregulation. Often, the initial balance needs to be recalibrated over time.

5.4 Risk of Fraud

The often-high value and electronic nature of emissions units as well as the architecture of the trading system make carbon spot markets especially prone to fraudulent activities. Factors that can affect the occurrence of fraud and losses include a system's design features, the coherence of its legal framework, and its administrative enforceability and oversight measures. Stringent regulations that can prevent and detect fraud and effectively enforce market rules are more easily achievable in national carbon markets, where trading is governed by one jurisdiction. The risk of fraud is especially predominant where the scope of the carbon market is not congruent with its levels of governance and oversight. This is the case in (i) regional carbon markets covered by different jurisdictions, such as the EU ETS, as some governance is at the EU level (e.g., registry) while some of it is at the national level (e.g., account opening), (ii) national markets that are directly linked, as in the case of the California and Québec carbon markets, and (iii) markets that are indirectly linked through the use of international emission certificates such as CDM or JI units. Furthermore, in general, the higher the carbon price, the more attractive the carbon market is for fraudsters (Bussmann, 2020).

The following types of fraud can occur:

5.4.1 Value-Added Tax (VAT) Fraud

VAT fraud is a highly complex type of fraud, in which organized criminal groups divert public resources. It can occur if the amount of VAT charged on allowance transfers, or the method or the tax authority collecting it are not uniform within a carbon market (Nield and Pereira, 2016). There are two ways VAT fraudsters specializing in cross-border trades can exploit the weaknesses of heterogeneous tax regimes and gaps in market oversight: (i) missing-trader fraud and (ii) VAT carousel fraud.

In the case of missing-trader fraud, the perpetrator acquires emission allowances from another jurisdiction where they are exempted from VAT and sells them in their jurisdiction, where VAT applies, charging the domestic VAT to buyers without remitting the VAT to the tax authority. The fraudster disappears before the fraud is discovered, thereby becoming the "missing trader" (see Figure 9).

In the more complex case of the VAT carousel, fraudsters build a network of interconnected companies located in different jurisdictions within the same carbon market, as depicted in Figure 9. To disguise the fraud, allowances are transferred along long chains of transactions through buffer companies and in a circle across borders multiple times. In each trading cycle, the importer of the allowances (i.e., the missing trader) does not return the VAT to the tax authority of the country where it is located. Moreover, each time an allowance is sold across a national border, the exporting trader (Company D), often part of the fraud network, illegitimately receives a VAT refund from the respective tax authority (Europol, 2009). This cycle can be repeated several times. Depending on the amount of VAT charged on allowances, the financial damage for the governments involved can be considerable.

A landmark case of VAT fraud occurred in the EU ETS in 2008 and 2009.[14] Emission allowances were treated as a supply of services, so that VAT was charged on the transfer of allowances. Fraudsters had an easy time in a market encompassing several jurisdictions where VAT provisions and collection are regulated at the country level, leading to a situation where fraudsters could exploit the loopholes of a patchwork of governance structures. Their actions generated losses of more than EUR 5 billion in public funds across several countries (Europol, 2009).

In April 2010, the scheme was finally stopped after a large-scale investigation conducted by the German authorities. Some 230 offices and homes, as well as a total of 150 suspects at 50 different companies, came under investigation, including German energy giant RWE AG and Deutsche Bank.[15] The missing traders in such VAT frauds are shell companies that usually exist for a few

---

[14] www.france24.com/en/20180129-france-trial-carbon-credits-fraud-paris-crime-emissions-scam-melgrani-marseille.

[15] www.spiegel.de/wirtschaft/unternehmen/razzia-bei-deutscher-bank-verdacht-auf-betrug-mit-co2-zertifikaten-a-872448.html.

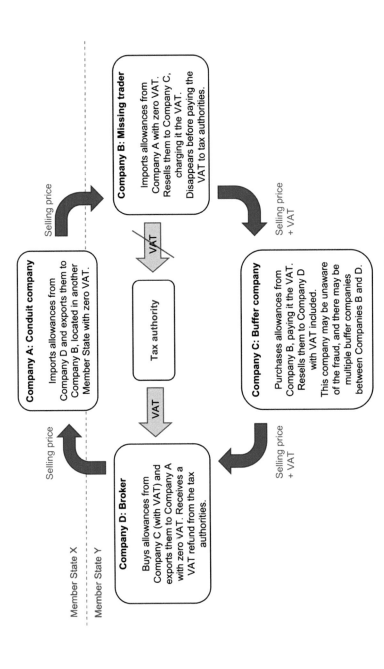

Figure 9 Missing trader VAT fraud

Source: Own graphic based on Nield and Pereira (2016).

months only (Borselli, 2011). An analysis of EU ETS transaction data reveals that more than half of the fraudulent volumes had been transferred by missing traders whose trading accounts were registered in Denmark, although those companies were not situated in Denmark. This suggests that the Danish registry had the loophole that enabled fraudsters to open trading accounts without the need for documentation of identity – at least during those early years of the ETS, after which such loopholes were closed in an uncoordinated way over time in the individual countries. Figure 10 shows that the fraudsters moved their operations to the Italian registry in 2010 as Italy was very late in adjusting national VAT regulations.

5.4.2 Money Laundering

Carbon markets can be misused to launder the profits from criminal activities such as VAT fraud. Typically, the illicit source of money is concealed in three stages (Williams, 2013): (i) placement (entry of money in the market by purchasing allowances), (ii) layering (long trading chains through sub-accounts to disguise the connection of allowances to illegal proceeds), and (iii) integration (recapturing the illicit proceeds by selling the allowances).

The primary market (spot trading) is especially at risk because anti–money laundering (AML) regulations are often missing, while secondary markets and dealing with derivatives are often covered in existing financial market regulation that includes AML provisions.

Experts have long warned against money laundering in carbon markets. Crime networks that operate in many markets for different products track and exploit loopholes in vulnerable carbon markets. They constantly develop new methods to circumvent existing regulations and hide illegal proceeds. Money laundering often occurs conjointly with other types of fraud. This was the case in the EU ETS, where criminal networks were found guilty for both VAT fraud and money laundering.[16]

5.4.3 Tax Evasion

Tax evasion can occur when a company is at the same time covered by an ETS and involved in the generation of international carbon offsets used for compliance through investments in emission reduction projects (INTERPOL, 2013). This situation entails the risk that the company sets up a chain of subsidiary companies to manipulate the price of the carbon certificate to avoid the payment

---

[16] www.euractiv.com/section/energy/news/polish-broker-faces-seven-year-prison-sentence-for-vat-fraud-on-eu-carbon-market/.

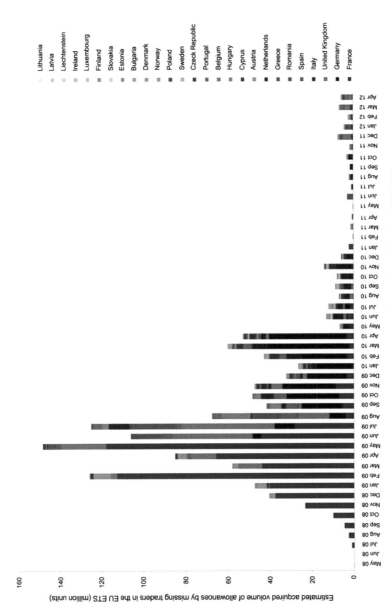

Figure 10 Development of VAT fraud in the EU ETS

Source: Wei (2016).

of taxes on profits from the generation of credits. Instead of directly buying the carbon certificate at market price from the subsidiary company generating the certificate, it purchases the certificate through an intermediary based in a location where no tax applies (tax haven). The subsidiary company evades taxes by selling the certificate to the intermediary below value. The intermediary then resells the credits to the parent company tax-free and at a higher price.

The Swedish newspaper *Dagens Nyheter* has reported about such cases of alleged tax evasion in the EU ETS.[17]

5.4.4 Allowance Theft

Theft of allowances is a form of fraud where the fraudster gains control over an account in an emissions trading registry through "phishing" for account access information or through more aggressive cyber-hacking methods. Phishers deceive account holders via emails to disclose identification numbers and passwords and subsequently issue unauthorized transfers of allowances. The possibility of allowance theft not only shows the vulnerability of the techno-logical infrastructure and low level of security of the registry; it also reveals the legal risks of participating in the trade of emission allowances. The theft can cause uncertainty about valid ownership and liability of purchasers of stolen allowances. Market participants are exposed to the risk of purchasing stolen allowances that will have to be returned without compensation, so good-faith buyers risk losing their initial investments (Nield and Pereira, 2016). While the legal principle of good faith would suggest that innocent buyers deserve protection in such cases, an absence of clear legal rules can lead to uncertainty about whether the damage will have to be borne by the buyer or by the account holder from which the allowances have been stolen.

From 2010 to 2011, the EU ETS witnessed a series of phishing and hacking attacks that targeted accounts in the Austrian, Czech, Greek, Romanian, and Italian registries. More than two million allowances were stolen, and the theft could be stopped only when the European Commission (EC) suspended spot trading. Not all stolen allowances could be traced and returned. In a lawsuit against the EC, the EU Court of Justice decided that the cement giant Lafarge Holcim, whose account was hacked, had to bear the damage of the fraud.[18] The EC further decided to reduce uncertainty for good-faith buyers by allowing the stolen allowances to be resold and by deleting the serial numbers of allowances, so that they can no longer be differentiated. This step has come at the cost of

---

[17] www.atmosfair.de/en/offsetting-from-tax-havens/.
[18] www.reuters.com/article/uk-holcim-carbon-idUKKCN0HS1E720141003.

making the market less transparent, because it is no longer possible to follow the trade of a single unit (Williams, 2013; Nield and Pereira, 2016).

5.4.5 Selling Fake Credits or Allowances

The risk of buying fake certificates exists in both cap-and-trade and baseline-and-credit systems, although manipulating the system and creating invalid certificates are easier in certain baseline-and-credit markets, where there is limited surveillance, international coverage, and no coherent governance structures (as is the case in much of the voluntary market). Frequently, information about the multiple types of accepted credits and about the reliability of the different markets available is often difficult for a buyer to gauge. The risk ranges from lax MRV processes that lead to the verification and generation of certificates from non-additional projects (see Section 3.3) to falsifying of the emission reduction project itself. While the civil law principles of estoppel and good faith – as reflected in statutory and customary law – could offer some protection to prospective buyers of fraudulent credits, there are often limits to their practical enforcement, for instance when the (fraudulent) seller is no longer reachable or the seller's assets have been frozen or confiscated. In practice, buyer protection provided by financial intermediaries such as brokers and clearing platforms plays a more important role.

Cases of fake credits have been reported in white certificate systems in Italy and France (Di Santo et al., 2018). In the Italian case, ill-purpose companies with parent companies located outside Italy were created to present false projects by providing false documentation in the range of 600,000 certificates. Some 700,000 additional certificates were blocked after more detailed checks. The reduction of 1.3 million certificates caused a collapse in supply. As a result, the price of certificates more than doubled. The Italian Ministry of Economic Development temporarily reduced spot market sessions to one per month and introduced a price cap, which had the desired effect of calming down the certificate price.

5.4.6 Impact on Efficiency and Environmental Integrity

The immediate effect of fraud is monetary damage, which can be severe. In the case of the VAT fraud carousels (see above), criminal activity causes not only loss of tax revenue but also the theft of state funds. Depending on the amount of VAT that is charged on allowances, the financial damage for governments can be large.

Fraud can also have a severe negative effect on market efficiency. VAT fraud, for example, can cause a surprising and unnaturally sharp increase in transactions and the volume of allowances traded. In the EU ETS, fraud caused the number of transactions to increase by a factor of 10, which dropped and normalized only after the detection and stop of the VAT fraud carousels (Frunza et al., 2011). As a result, the behavior of fraudsters, rather than market fundamentals, can determine allowance prices, which no longer reflect the marginal abatement costs and impair the efficiency of the carbon market (Nield and Pereira, 2016). Once such fraudulent activities are detected and the market has been informed, there is a crippling effect on trust in the market, leading to reduced trading volumes and lower market liquidity.

VAT fraud or money laundering, which do not affect the number of allowances traded, have no direct impact on the environmental integrity. However, other types of fraud, such as the creation and sale of fake credits, which can be used to offset emissions, inflate the cap unnaturally and ultimately lead to an increase in global emissions (see Section 4.2).

5.4.7 Prevention, Detection, and Enforcement

An important requirement for the prevention of fraud is restricting access to the market and the registry. As Nield and Pereira (2016) pointed out, excluding account holders whose purpose for holding an account was unclear was an effective method for fraud prevention in the Danish Registry. Furthermore, the need to provide proof of identity, bank and VAT details, and applicants' criminal record upon opening of registry accounts is another crucial requirement. Based on the information provided, stringent security measures and know-your-customer (KYC) checks should be applied. Access to the market should be denied to convicted and suspected criminals (Nield and Pereira, 2016).

Centralizing market governance and trading can facilitate market oversight. To this end, a centralized registry should be created as well as an official trading platform that acts as a central marketplace and renders transactions even more secure. Mandatory reporting on transactions and holdings are important additional market oversight measures.

Many risks arise from the scattered legal basis and from unclear or conflicting responsibilities in a fragmented governance system. At the very first stage of designing a carbon market, it is therefore necessary to ensure coherent market oversight and adopt market rules that can be enforced across the entire market. For example, the risk of VAT fraud can be mitigated by a uniform VAT system within the entire carbon market. If the market is spread across various jurisdictions and a unified VAT system is not feasible, it must be ensured that the differences in VAT from cross-border transfers are coherently addressed across all jurisdictions. The EU countries did not coordinate actions in the fight against fraud in 2008–2009. Different measures were therefore taken in each country, which caused the fraudulent activities to shift to jurisdictions that had not adapted their domestic VAT regulations yet (e.g., Italy).

Experiences with the EU ETS have shown that if the buyer is responsible for remitting the tax on cross-border trades of emission allowances, the system is vulnerable to VAT fraud. Placing the liability of paying the VAT with the supplier of the allowances in an approach called "reverse charge mechanism," can mitigate the risk of VAT fraud and has been applied by many EU countries as an interim measure (Kogels, 2010). An even more effective way to prevent VAT fraud, however, would be to completely exempt the trade of allowances from VAT. This could be achieved by defining allowances as a financial product rather than a commodity.

Reducing complexity can be an important step toward reducing fraudulent activities, such as by restricting the creation of complex financial products with allowances. Classifying allowances as financial products can also help to prevent money laundering within the spot market as financial market regulation and oversight will be applied. However, money laundering activities involving carbon offset creation can still occur as the origins of offsets may lay outside of the regulated territory (Williams, 2013).

Finally, fraud has been associated with shell companies in tax havens such as Hong Kong, the United Arab Emirates, Switzerland, and Singapore. When companies located outside the EU create accounts in the European emissions trading register, fraud and tax evasion can become much more difficult to prevent or detect due to a lack of effective cooperation between EU and non-EU authorities. Therefore, another way to prevent fraud may be restricting the companies eligible to trade in cap-and-trade markets. This is done in Korea, where only regulated entities and banks with special permission have access to the market. The increased security provided by restricting market access, however, comes to the detriment of market liquidity, which in turn affects efficiency as markets with low trading volumes are prone to greater price volatility.

While preventative measures are the best way to avoid abuse and losses, market creators should adopt measures that make the detection of fraud and suspicious trades quick and effective. Rapid detection is important to keep the damage caused by potential fraud attacks to a minimum and to deter fraudsters. While the integration of adequate anti–money laundering regulations into the carbon market helps to detect and prevent both money laundering and fraud, effective detection often stands and falls with the existence of a complete, reliable, and transparent database with detailed information on account holders and transactions.

Regular data analysis using appropriate algorithms can help speed up detection. More stringent regulation of financial market oversight has led to the development of data mining techniques for fraud detection that could also be applied in carbon markets. However, trustworthy real-time trade and account data are an essential requirement.

Finally, effective law enforcement action against fraud in carbon markets requires coherent and harmonized market governance as well as the necessary resources, both in law enforcement and in the judiciary. This also includes harmonization of the legal framework concerning the valid ownership of allowances and clear rules on the liability of inadvertent purchasers of fraudulent units. Without these measures in place, detected fraud and related crimes are difficult to prosecute and punish, causing new problems for the authorities and the damaged parties.

5.5 Risk of Corruption

Corruption can affect both cap-and-trade and baseline-and-credit systems. Cap-and-trade systems are particularly prone to corruption at the stage when the regulation is being developed or when trading takes place at the government level. However, there are also specific processes where the risk of corruption is particularly high. To hide underreporting or to avoid sanctions, companies may corrupt verifiers or government officials by offering bribes.

While Buen and Michaelowa (2009) found that the CDM, at least in its early years, did not face significant allegations of corruption, opportunities for corruption clearly exist in various areas of baseline-and-credit systems, given that verifiers and regulators are involved in the day-to-day approval of projects and issuance of credits.

5.5.1 Examples of Corruption

There are some examples of bribery in cap-and-trade systems at the international level. In 2008, for example, the Slovak government sold around 15 million AAUs to a U.S.-based company, Interblue Group, at EUR 5.05/ AAU – when prices were around twice as high. The media and political opposition criticized the fact that the allowances had been sold below the actual market price and that the government had used neither tender nor auction to sell them but, rather, had allocated them to Interblue Group directly. The evidence suggested that corruption had occurred. The scandal led to the dismissal of at least two ministers as the AAUs were resold directly for EUR 8 or more per AAU, leading to a profit of at least EUR 45 million.[19]

Other examples related to baseline-and-credit systems at the international regulatory level show that regulators may be bribed to take specific actions in

---

[19] https://blog.transparency.org/2011/06/03/emissions-trading-and-bribery-investigations-in-slovakia/index.html.

favor of a project or program. At the national level, regulators approving activities may accept a bribe to give their approval. National-level officials may divert revenues from credit sales. Auditors may be bribed to issue a favorable validation or verification report, experts may be bribed not to submit critical comments at validation, and local stakeholders may want a bribe in exchange for positive comments (Dobson, 2015).

Wood and colleagues (2016) quoted various project developers implying that it was necessary to bribe the Tanzanian CDM approval authority. CDM project developers in Vietnam have also reported that there is a clearly communicated bribe "tariff" for getting an approval letter, as described by Nguyen and colleagues (2011). One of the authors of this volume (Axel Michaelowa) was offered a bribe by an Indian CDM consultancy to write a positive report on the Toranagallu steel project (see Section 3.3.1) after he had made a public comment to the validator regarding the lack of additionality.

5.5.2 Prevention, Detection, and Enforcement

The more transparency is required, the lower the scope for corruption. Transactions involving governments require transparency in terms of both the process and prices. In baseline-and-credit systems, meetings of regulatory authorities should be held in the presence of observers. All relevant documents regarding regulatory decisions should be published. The members of international and national bodies approving projects should be selected based on professional competence rather than their representation of geographical areas or stakeholder groups. They should also be required to state their current and previous roles and potential conflicts of interest in detail in a publicly available document (Buen and Michaelowa, 2009). Regulatory requirements should be defined as specifically as possible to reduce regulatory leeway that might facilitate corruption.

6 Toward Effective Market Oversight

6.1 Lessons Learned from Existing Markets for Improving Governance Arrangements for Carbon Markets

Throughout this volume, we have reviewed a series of risks to the environmental integrity and economic efficiency of carbon markets. A key finding has been that those risks become larger when different markets – with diverse sets of rules, authorities, and participating entities – are connected to each other. This is in line with the findings of the literature on multilevel and polycentric governance arrangements: Decentralized authority bears the risks of insufficient, patchy, and uncoordinated regulation (Bailey and Maresh, 2009; Biermann et al., 2009).

How, then, can such governance arrangements for carbon markets be made more robust to loopholes, abuses, and even organized crime?

One crucial aspect is transparency. Transparency is vital for the appropriate functioning of all types of carbon markets, including the trading phase, and to reduce the risk of corruption.

In the past, sufficient, up-to-date, and reliable data on emission trends for different sectors and industries, and on the emission benchmarks of specific technologies, were crucial within individual markets in order to set a stringent cap and establish credible baselines. In particular, it was important for statistical offices to provide reliable data on past emissions and production output to allow a range of independent assessments on future trends and baseline scenarios. This should become easier in the future, where a zero target is the long-term aim, as only the emissions path from today's emissions level to zero emissions at an appropriate "net zero date" needs to be defined. Once this path has been defined, the dispute over the correct projections becomes obsolete.

Transparency – and suitable, secure infrastructure to ensure it – is also key to avoid fraud and abuse in trading allowances. The best way to prevent or detect fraud in market transactions is to provide reliable real-time data on transfers for each account, covering not only spot but also derivate markets. Experience shows that not all regulators are willing to allow such transparency: Transparency provisions have often been overridden by arguing confidentiality concerns on cost information for new technologies or to protect buyers from liability after buying fraudulent allowances. This has led to quite different provisions on transparency for market transactions in different countries. In some countries, the disaggregated data is published only three to five years after the fact, which makes it impossible for experts to monitor what is happening in the market. If data are not timely and publicly available, market activity cannot be monitored sufficiently. A lack of transparency leads to a creeping erosion of the market's stringency because problems and abuses are not discovered and addressed.

Preventing fraud such as double-issuance and double-use of carbon market units requires robust registries and transaction logs, including monitoring of transactions between exchanges and across different markets. When linking markets, therefore, provisions need to be made for sharing information between the regulators of the participating markets in real time, ideally by creating a common registry. Registries need to be secure to prevent hacking and theft, for example, by ensuring registry account security through KYC checks.

The problems caused by a lack of transparency may be compounded by **insufficient staffing** of regulators. In the EU ETS, for example, the staff of national-level regulators (for example, the German Emissions Trading Authority [DEHSt] with around 160 employees[20]) is much larger than the staff in the offices of the overall regulator in Brussels (the section on European and International Carbon Markets at the Directorate-General for Climate Action, with 68 staff members[21]). This is again a problem of multilevel governance, with national-level units often having larger budgets than those at the supranational level. In the EU ETS, many administrative tasks such as the registry and allocation of allowances have been moved from the national to the European level, but the number of staff seems not to reflect those changes.

If more staffing is allocated to the higher market level rather than to individual country regulators, then policy, monitoring, and enforcement can be made more consistent. In addition, insufficient staff means that the regulator itself has limited capacities to monitor market transactions, detect irregularities, and act on them. At the opposite extreme, overstaffing can also become a problem, as the experience with the CDM staff at the UNFCCC Secretariat has shown. There, the unexpected level of resources from the administration fee levied on project registration and credit issuance led to an increase in staffing and influence exerted by the Secretariat on regulatory decisions (Michaelowa and Michaelowa, 2017). At some point, this may become inappropriate. The resulting governance issue is, therefore, to find the right staff size – and to allocate a sufficiently large budget to finance it – without falling victim to Parkinson's law of growing bureaucracies.

A third, crucial, governance aspect, particularly in supranational and inter-linked markets, is the **compatibility of legislation**, regulations, and even industrial structures, and the handling of unforeseen regulatory **loopholes** due to incompatibilities or changes in one of the systems. When loopholes exist and compatibility is lacking, the risk of abuse or fraud is correspondingly higher.

A fourth governance aspect is related to the public law principle of legality. It requires for market **rules and provisions to be properly specified to be enforceable.** One example is the case of supplementarity of the use of offsets, which was recognized as an important principle to avoid watering down emission targets under the Kyoto Protocol. Even though supplementarity is mentioned in the Kyoto Protocol in three places, and although it was discussed at length in the subsequent negotiations, an acceptable or allowed level for a party's use of Kyoto units was never agreed. The practical result is that it

---

[20] www.umweltbundesamt.de/das-uba/wer-wir-sind/organisation/fachbereich-v.

[21] https://op.europa.eu/en/web/who-is-who/organization/-/organization/CLIMA/COM_CRF_234712.

became impossible to enforce supplementarity, at least internationally, although this is a principle under the Kyoto Protocol.

Another example from the EU ETS is that there is a lack of information on how often spot checks on reported emissions are undertaken by authorities. Often, the exact fines issued for violations in case of detection are also unknown, which makes it impossible for companies to estimate the potential penalty. In addition, authorities believe that the cost of spot-checking small companies is likely to exceed the potential revenue from fines, which may encourage further criminal behavior from small companies.

Regulatory roles in carbon markets are frequently assumed by private actors. While this approach lightens the load of overburdened public officials, and while competition may increase the effectiveness of these private regulators, it may also lead to **conflict-of-interest situations**. In the EU ETS, for example, external advisers were not only involved in establishing the regulations, but they later also acted as verifiers of monitoring reports of participating installations. As a result, there is an incentive for these advisers to ensure that the rules they help design are more complicated than necessary as this may make their involvement in later assignments more extensive and, therefore, more profitable. Such situations have been observed in the Australian ETS process, where law firms were involved in writing the ETS bill, or in the EU ETS, where consultants drafted monitoring and verification guidelines.

Ideally, therefore, the consultants involved in establishing market rules should be different from those executing them. However, in a new market with relatively few experts, this may be difficult to achieve. This is why it is important for the authority to ensure the quality and integrity of verifiers through accreditation processes and spot checks by the authorities. Finally, to ensure an independent judgment, verification should be paid for by the authority rather than the regulated entity, and a rotation system for verification assignments should be introduced.

A final consideration relates to **dealing with unexpected circumstances** and crises. Frequently, regulators react to a crisis by relaxing certain rules to help the market cope with the situation. An example of this are the new baseline rules under CORSIA to deal with the effects of the coronavirus crisis on the aviation sector. When such requirements are relaxed, there is a risk that they become sticky and remain in place if there is no clear plan for going back to the stricter regulations once the crisis is overcome. This might reduce environmental effectiveness in the long term. Measures in reaction to a crisis should, therefore, always include provisions dealing with the end of that crisis.

In the next sections, we provide an overview of future challenges of carbon markets. We start with a medium-term perspective focusing on the international negotiations around Article 6 of the Paris Agreement and on voluntary carbon markets. Article 6 is still highly contested, and no agreement on detailed rules has been reached at the time of writing. International rules may become even more important in the long term when countries need to achieve the net-zero targets required by the Paris Agreement. Since suitable storage capacities or other prerequisites for successful implementation of negative emissions technologies vary substantially between countries, carbon markets are likely to continue playing a role in the long term. In the final section, we present our thoughts on likely amendments to and open research questions about carbon markets in a net-zero world.

6.2 Challenges for International Carbon Markets under the Paris Agreement

Article 6 of the Paris Agreement refers to two types of international markets. Article 6.2 allows countries to cooperate without any international oversight other than principles and certain reporting requirements. This is akin to the first track of JI and likely to generate similar problems as discussed in Section 3. Given that there are no limitations to the type of activities, collaboration under Article 6.2 may include transboundary or linked cap-and-trade systems as well as baseline-and-credit systems. By contrast, the Article 6.4 Mechanism is subject to international regulation through a supervisory body (SB). It is a baseline-and-credit system building on experiences from the CDM and the second track of JI. Both markets will generate internationally transferred mitigation outcomes (ITMOs).

According to our own analysis, out of 88 countries that had submitted updated NDCs to the UNFCCC by end of July 2021, 68 countries, or 77 percent, have explicitly stated that they want to use Article 6. Five of those have declared they only want to buy ITMOs, while another five are open to both buying and selling. Forty-two countries have clearly stated to aim at selling only, while 16 do not provide a clear statement. So, currently there is a clear imbalance between supply and demand.

Our discussion needs to be seen against the backdrop of the detailed rules for Article 6, which were only decided at COP26 in late 2021. Many details will need to be worked out over the next few years, as experience with the CDM suggests. There are, therefore, many opportunities to take into account the key lessons learned from past markets.

The intense calls to prevent double-claiming (see Section 5.2) led to a robust accounting system with corresponding adjustments without exceptions to ensure that any ITMOs sold to other countries or entities are not counted toward the host country's own target. As long as the NDC target is more stringent than business-as-usual emissions, this is a good safeguard to prevent Article 6.2 generating ITMOs with low environmental integrity. Problems arise if the NDC target is not binding, which would generate hot air. As shown in Section 3, absence of international oversight here is likely to lead to manipulation of international carbon markets. This means that the detailed reporting requirements, which are still under negotiation in 2022, need to be as detailed and transparent as possible to enable NGOs and other stakeholders to recognize signs of manipulation and raise the alarm (Michaelowa et al., 2020b). Moreover, UNFCCC expert review teams should be given a strong mandate to uncover manipulation in monitoring reports and to request countries to adjust their programs. However, under Article 6.2, the key reporting will take place on an aggregated, jurisdictional level rather than in terms of individual activities. In the CDM, aggregated reporting became much less transparent than originally envisaged due to strong lobbying of credit buyers based on competitiveness concerns, which led various jurisdictions to withhold disaggregated data on transactions of CDM credits (Michaelowa et al., 2021a). The reporting and transparency rules for the Article 6.2 mechanism therefore need to be as disaggregated as possible to enable identification and elimination of problematic credits.

The second-best approach to ensuring that Article 6.2 does not lead to manipulation would be the formation of clubs of seller and buyer countries which would agree to adhere to minimum standards. The first club of this type was a group of 32 countries underwriting the "San José Principles for High Ambition and Integrity in International Carbon Markets" orchestrated by Switzerland and Costa Rica in December 2019.[22] So far, however, the operationalization of these principles remains unclear. For example, the Swiss KliK foundation, in its public calls for Article 6 pilot activity submissions, applies relatively broad criteria, which are susceptible to manipulation and abuse and certainly no better than the criteria for validation under the CDM. In contrast to that, Sweden has hired the Gold Standard to certify all Article 6.2 ITMOs. Given that the Gold Standard has built its reputation on generating high integrity credits, this safeguard mechanism is likely to work.

The principles to ensure environmental integrity under the Article 6.4 Mechanism are quite strong. For the first time, the additionality definition makes sense, requiring to show that "the activity would not have occurred in the absence of the incentives from the mechanism." All relevant national policies need to be considered and locking in "levels of emissions, technologies

---

[22] https://cambioclimatico.go.cr/sanjoseprinciples/about-the-san-jose-principles/.

or carbon-intensive practices" is to be prevented. Baselines shall be set below business-as-usual, and need to be aligned to the long-term targets of the Paris Agreement. This allows application of the concept of an "ambition coefficient" (Michaelowa et al., 2021b; see also Section 6.3).

In operationalizing these principles in the next years, the rich lessons learned while developing baseline and monitoring methodologies need to be incorporated. Given that developing new Article 6 methodologies from scratch would take many years and be costly (Michaelowa et al., 2020a estimated that the development of one new methodology requires USD 0.1–0.2 million), an International Initiative for Development of Article 6 Methodology Tools (II-AMT) was launched in 2022, with a group of international methodology experts from all continents to generate tools that can be added to Kyoto mechanism baseline and monitoring methodologies in a modular fashion (Perspectives, 2022). Such Article 6 tools will contain clear definitions of key concepts serving as guidance on what to consider for alignment with host countries' climate and sustainable development priorities. Guidance will also be included on how to consider existing and planned policies in additionality determination and baseline setting as well as on different concepts related to "conditionality" in NDC targets. The tools will support the alignment of Article 6 activities with the NDC implementation periods and ensure an update of key parameters in reference scenarios and crediting baselines in line with both these implementation periods and the pace of technological change and innovation in different sectors.

The tools will also facilitate reporting by the host country on how its engagement in Article 6 cooperation contributes to NDC implementation, prevents new burdens such as those generated by selling off "low-hanging fruit," and fosters sustainable development. They aim at redefining and reconceptualizing the concept of additionality to cover three "shades" of additionality: financial additionality (going beyond a commercially viable business-as-usual project), regulatory additionality (not being mandated by law or regulation), and target additionality (not being required for host country achievement of (unconditional) NDC targets). While striving for high integrity, the tools aim to be practical in nature and be no undue burden for project developers. Their development will be accompanied by a thorough assessment of their applicability in different country contexts and of related transaction costs.

Host country stakeholders will play a key role in governing both Articles 6.4 and 6.2. This entails risks regarding the manipulation of baseline and additionality determination as well as corruption in the context of authorization. Thus, building up the capacity of host country institutions, consultants, and activity developers to deal with issues related to the Article 6 mechanisms and addressing potential conflicts of interest through appropriate mechanism design (e.g., transparent tenders or rewards for discovering abuse) is crucial to prevent loss of environmental integrity. Moreover, seller country governments need to be enabled to consider the opportunity costs of selling ITMOs due to corresponding adjustments when assessing the benefits obtained from Article 6 cooperation. Such an understanding improves policymakers' judgment of the appropriateness of prices paid for credits, which reduces corruption risks.

Another crucial issue is the link between Article 6 and voluntary carbon markets. While any ITMO will be subject to corresponding adjustments, non-authorized Article 6.4 emission reductions will not. Currently, an intense debate is ongoing among voluntary carbon market stakeholders regarding the need for corresponding adjustments for internationally transferred credits. This now leads to two potential approaches for voluntary market stakeholders as shown in **Figure 11** whereas the potential uses of credits from the voluntary carbon market depend on whether they implement corresponding adjustments or not.

According to the International Carbon Reduction and Offset Alliance (ICROA), corresponding adjustments are unnecessary because "carbon reductions financed by the [voluntary carbon market] are not exported from the host country" and "voluntary activity does not lead to double counting at the UN level because carbon reductions are recorded only once by the country hosting the mitigation activity" (ICROA, 2020: 1), and not by the country where the

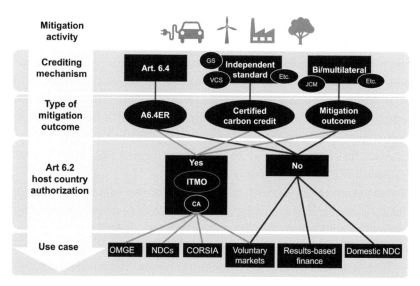

Figure 11 The two possible approaches for the voluntary market under Article 6

Source: Michaelowa (2021). CA = Corresponding adjustment; OMGE = Overall Mitigation in Global Emissions; GS = Gold Standard; VCS = Voluntary Carbon Standard; JCM = Joint Crediting Mechanism. Any use of ITMOs requires corresponding adjustments. But voluntary market credits may continue to be transferred outside the Article 6 infrastructure.

buyer company resides. The largest voluntary carbon market standard provider Verra supports a similar view.

A company buying voluntary credits will, of course, use them to offset emissions in its home country to prevent becoming subject to a mandatory mitigation policy. If a mitigation outcome is counted toward a host country NDC target as well as claimed to offset emissions caused elsewhere, this is a clear case of double-claiming. This causes the argument of ICROA and Verra to crumble, which is acknowledged by the Gold Standard (2021). It should be stressed that voluntary carbon markets can contribute to enhancing global mitigation only when they incentivize mitigation beyond host country commitments and contribute to closing the "ambition gap" that characterizes most current NDCs. If voluntary carbon markets are not adjusted for accordingly, there is a high risk that host countries will fail to implement mitigation policy instruments to the extent that would otherwise be necessary to achieve the NDC targets.

6.3 Open Research Questions: How to Make Carbon Markets Consistent with a Net-Zero World

In addition to the still not fully resolved issues concerning Article 6 and voluntary carbon markets, there are many open questions as to how carbon markets can be made compatible with a net-zero world. Article 4 of the Paris Agreement states "that a balance between anthropogenic emissions by sources and removals by sinks of greenhouse gases in the second half of this century" is necessary "in order to achieve the long-term temperature goal." To achieve net-zero targets or GHG neutrality by 2050, the IPCC (2018) and the IEA (2021) refer to substantial investments in carbon capture and storage (CCS) and carbon dioxide removal (CDR) to offset the difficult-to-reduce GHGs from agriculture, industrial processes, and aviation. The IPCC also foresees CDR for emission overshoots that would otherwise take the planet beyond the carbon budgets consistent with a 1.5°C temperature target.

Baseline-and-credit systems face specific challenges in a net-zero world: What, for example, is an appropriate approach to baseline setting for emissions reductions? Ensuring that the baseline is in line with achieving the long-term temperature goal of the Paris Agreement and with host countries' long-term Low Emissions and Development Strategies or carbon neutrality commitments requires bold new approaches. Baselines defined in intensity terms (volume of GHGs per unit of production of a good or service), as has been the norm under existing baseline-and-credit mechanisms, create the problem that even if the emission intensity falls substantially, and credits are allocated for such a reduction, overall emissions fall much less or may even rise because production levels increase.

So far, it has been argued that such an approach is important to address the "suppressed demand" for goods and services in poor countries. For this reason, the application of an emission intensity approach needs to be allowed to continue. It must, however, be combined with an "ambition coefficient" to ensure that, at the point in time where emissions are to reach net zero, any baseline for emission reduction activities also reaches zero. The most straightforward approach for such an ambition coefficient is to define an emissions path from today's emissions level to zero emissions at an appropriate "net-zero date" for each host country of a baseline-and-credit mechanism (Michaelowa et al., 2021b). Applying the principle of common, but differentiated, responsibilities means that the net-zero date for industrialized countries would be quite soon, probably in the 2030s. For least developed countries (LDCs), the net-zero date would of course be much later, perhaps around 2070. At each point in time, the ambition coefficient would be equal to the percentage of today's emissions reached for that specific year on the downward sloping path, reaching zero in the net-zero year. This approach is depicted in Figure 12.

In the context of Article 6.2, buyer clubs could decide on the appropriate level of ambition coefficient, while for Article 6.4, this decision could be taken by its Supervisory Board. Ambition coefficients cannot be manipulated openly; obviously, the process of setting the net-zero year is vulnerable to corruption. As suggested above, a transparent approach would reduce this risk.

Dealing with countries whose emissions deviate increasingly from the ambition-compatible path would be challenging as emissions continue, while related emission reductions cannot create any more credits. This generates

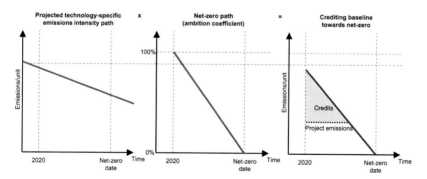

Figure 12 Application of an ambition coefficient toward a net-zero world

Source: Own graphic based on Michaelowa and colleagues (2021b). The ambition coefficient would be differentiated according to level of development.

a strong incentive problem. Naming and shaming them will probably not be sufficient to bring these countries on track.

The situation is different if we assess what changes are necessary to cap-and-trade systems. To understand what is traded in a net-zero world, we first look at the technological and biological options to achieve negative emissions. Figure 13 classifies the removal options and compares them with today's common emission reduction approaches, showing how they have been covered by carbon markets so far. This allows us to understand the types of incentive that already exist and what types still need to be developed. Cap-and-trade systems give industrial plants or fossil fuel power plants an incentive to invest in CCS as they allow companies to buy fewer CO_2 allowances and even to sell allowances if they have received free allocation. However, this would lead only to negative emissions if the burned fuel is biogenic; otherwise, it will only lead to zero emissions.

As natural CO_2 sinks due to afforestation and reforestation or sequestration in the soil have usually not been covered by cap-and-trade systems – except in New Zealand – they may be included in offsetting systems. Such CDR options involve taking CO_2 from the atmosphere and binding it in charcoal (biochar) or storing it in vegetation or in the soil. These natural sinks are relatively inexpensive, and there is ample experience in dealing with them. However, such storage is short-lived, and there is a high risk of reversal when forest fires or other events release the CO_2 back into the atmosphere. This risk needs to be considered when designing an offset market with natural carbon removal.

Baseline-and-credit systems may also provide incentives for investments in removal technologies that allow CO_2 to be captured directly from the atmosphere and stored in suitable facilities underground. This process is called direct air-carbon capture and storage (DACCS). In order to achieve permanence, the captured CO_2 can be dissolved in water which is pumped into basaltic rock. In about two years the CO_2 mineralizes in pores of the basalt and is therefore stored very safely. Negative emissions can also be achieved by using biomass for energy production – green methane – and subsequently storing the CO_2 emissions in a process called "bioenergy with CCS" (BECCS). A risk of BECCS that would need to be addressed by the offset market is the probability of increased emissions when biomass production leads to additional forest clearance.

Insurance and buffers are options for addressing the risks of reversal and leakage under baseline-and-credit systems (see Section 4.2.3).

For the removal of GHGs, the baseline methodologies could continue to apply the current approaches until countries take up "net-negative" targets that involve achieving a specific amount of GHG removal. Once negative targets are

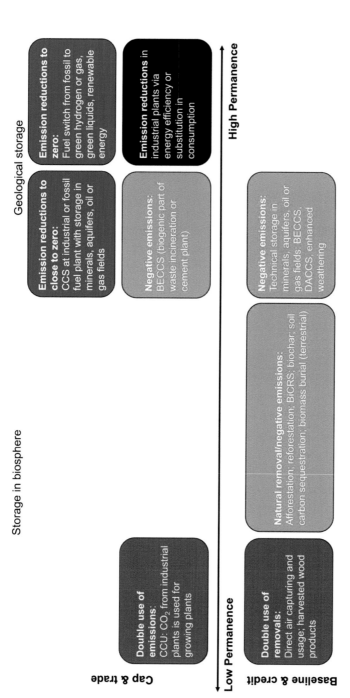

Figure 13 Carbon removal options in a net-zero world

Source: Own graphic. Green relates to negative emissions, blue to zero or near-zero emissions, black to reduction compared to a baseline situation, and red indicates that there may be temporary sequestration but that at the end of the usage process the carbon is emitted into the atmosphere. BiCRS: Biomass Carbon Removal and Storage.

introduced, a new approach could be for removal activities to only become eligible for ITMO transfers once the domestic removal target has been achieved. That would, however, lead to strong swings in eligibility over time. An alternative would be to define a negative baseline at a removal intensity consistent with achieving the overall removal target within the relevant NDC period. This approach would generate a better incentive to continue to engage in the market. If removal takes a larger or even a monopoly role in international carbon markets, issues related to fraud regarding storage site MRV will become highly relevant.

As illustrated in Figure 13, most of the CDR technologies require CCS. As not all countries have suitable storage sites, and residents frequently react with resistance if CO_2 is to be stored on their doorstep, it is likely that storage will result in some international transfers with the captured CO_2 being stored offshore and in former gas and oil deposits, locations where the required infrastructure and technical knowledge are also already available. However, the transfer of CO_2 to distant locations results in long transport routes, and CO_2 leakage may well be a risk along the way, which would need to be addressed.

If capture, transport, and storage are covered by a cap-and-trade system, allowances covering any leakage would need to be surrendered, as is done in the EU ETS with CCS and in the New Zealand system with leakage or reversal in afforestation and reforestation.

Direct air capturing with usage, harvested wood products, as well as carbon capture and usage (CCU) are further technologies that could help, at least temporarily, to shift emissions to the future. However, these options cannot reduce, avoid, or remove emissions permanently. Therefore, a different accounting method needs to be applied.

If carbon markets integrate CCS and removal units, the market will determine what technology will be deployed. As illustrated in Figure 14, as soon as classic abatement options including green hydrogen become more expensive than buying removal units from DACCS and BECCS (which function as backstop technologies), they will be replaced. The cheapest technologies will be used first. As a result, a market price will emerge. This must be high enough to finance negative emission technologies.

Given that CDR will require high carbon prices and that free allowance allocation is not possible in a net-zero world, carbon border adjustment mechanisms (CBAM) can help to reduce the impact on competition. Carbon markets could be integrated into such mechanisms; for example, an exemption from paying the CBAM rate by surrendering a removal or reduction credit could be granted.

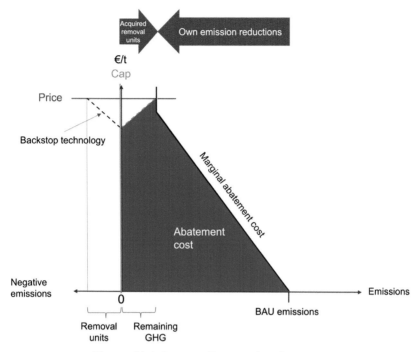

Figure 14 A "net-zero" cap-and-trade system

Source: Own graphic.

There are a number of open questions with regard to carbon markets under a net-zero target:

How are the current blueprints of carbon markets compatible with CDR as biomass plants, for instance, are usually not covered by cap-and-trade systems? Will there be a separate market for emissions removal units or will markets be integrated, and will they apply qualitative and quantitative restrictions? What will be the share of CDR and emissions reductions in achieving the net-zero targets if there are separate markets? Who should be awarded the removal unit, and how will the value be divided between capturer, transportation, and storage provider? How can co-risks such as land conflicts, food security, loss of biodiversity and co-benefits such as enhanced biodiversity be addressed and reflected adequately?

These are all questions that will need to be answered by future research on carbon markets.

6.4 Concluding Remarks

At this point, the reader may be somewhat overwhelmed by the complexity of designing carbon markets and all of the risks involved. Given that this volume focuses explicitly on such risks, this is not unexpected. One may be tempted to ask oneself, however, whether it is at all possible to design functioning carbon markets. Given that they are being adopted by a growing number of jurisdictions, however, carbon markets are probably here to stay. If designed well, they can be an important tool for closing the gap between the Paris Agreement's global mitigation goals and countries' NDCs.

As this volume has shown, carbon markets have given rise to regulatory challenges since their inception, yet the policy responses to these challenges have also matured and grown in sophistication over time. Studying the complex regulatory frameworks that have developed in existing cap-and-trade and baseline-and-credit systems can offer valuable lessons for the regulation of emerging and future carbon markets.

Regulatory challenges in these markets will continue to evolve, however, as the climate policy objectives they serve become more ambitious and converge around net-zero emissions, the value of traded units gradually increases, and markets become more interconnected, whether through bilateral linkage or multilateral cooperation frameworks such as Article 6 of the Paris Agreement. New digital tools, such as software-based analysis of market data and remote sensing for compliance control, may help manage these challenges as they become available and more widely used. Ultimately, however, the precise nature of such future challenges is difficult to predict.

In such a context of uncertainty, future decision-makers can derive guidance from the general principles of carbon market regulation set out at the beginning of this volume. At any rate, if carbon markets are to play a role in advancing the global effort to decarbonize our economies, sound regulation will only gain – not lose – in importance going forward.

References

Abrell, J., Cludius, J., Lehmann, S., Schleich, J., Betz, R., 2021. Corporate emissions-trading behaviour during the first decade of the EU ETS. *Environment and Resource Economics*, forthcoming. https://doi.org/10.1007/s10640-021-00593-7.

Acworth, W., Kuneman, E., forthcoming. *Influence of Market Structures and Market Regulation on the Carbon Market – Synthesis Report*. Dessau-Roßlau: Federal Environmental Agency.

Ahonen, H.-M., Kessler, J., Michaelowa, A., Espelage, A., Hoch, S., 2022. Governance of fragmented compliance and voluntary carbon markets under the Paris Agreement. *Politics and Governance*, 10(1), 235–245.

Bailey, I., Maresh, S., 2009. Scales and networks of neoliberal climate governance: The regulatory and territorial logics of European Union emissions trading. *Transactions of the Institute of British Geographers*, 34(4), 445–461.

Bel, G., Joseph, S., 2015. Emission abatement: Untangling the impacts of the EU ETS and the economic crisis. *Energy Economics*, 49, 531–539.

Betz, R., 2016. Emissions trading in practice: Lessons learnt from the European emissions trading scheme. In S. Managi (Ed.), *Handbook of Environmental Economics in Asia*. Abingdon: Routledge, 182–206.

Betz, R., Jones, M., MacGill, I., Passey, R., 2013. Trading in energy efficiency in Australia: What are the lessons learnt so far?. In T. L. Lindström (Ed.), *ECEEE Summer Study Proceedings on Energy Efficiency: Rethink, Renew, Restart*. Belambra Les Criques, France: European Council for an Energy Efficient Economy, 395–406.

Betz, R., Sato, M., 2006. Emissions trading: Lessons learnt from the 1st phase of EU ETS and prospects for the 2nd Phase. *Climate Policy*, 6(4), 351–359.

Biedenkopf, K., Müller, P., Slominski, P., Wettestad, J., 2017. A global turn to greenhouse gas emissions trading? Experiments, actors, and diffusion. *Global Environmental Politics*, 17(3), 1–11.

Biermann, F., Pattberg, P., van Asselt, H., Zelli, F., 2009. The fragmentation of global governance architectures: A framework for analysis. *Global Environmental Politics*, 9(4), 14–40.

Biermann, Frank. (2010). Beyond the intergovernmental regime: recent trends in global carbon governance. *Current Opinion in Environmental Sustainability*, 2(4), 284–288. DOI: 10.1016/j.cosust.2010.05.002

Black, H. C., 1990. *Black's Law Dictionary* (6th Ed.). St. Paul, MN: West.

Borenstein, S., Bushnell, J., Wolak, F. A., Zaragoza-Watkins, M., 2019. Expecting the unexpected: Emissions uncertainty and environmental market design. *American Economic Review*, 109(11), 3953–3977.

Borselli, F., 2011. *Organised VAT Fraud: Features, Magnitude, Policy Perspectives*. Bank of Italy Occasional Paper No. 106. Rome: Bank of Italy. https://doi.org/10.2139/ssrn.2023080.

Buen, J., Michaelowa, A., 2009. View from the inside – markets for carbon credits to fight climate change: Addressing corruption risks proactively. In Transparency International (Ed.), *Global Corruption Report 2009: Corruption and the Private Sector*. Cambridge: Cambridge University Press, 41–45.

Burtraw, D., McCormack, K., 2016. *Consignment Auctions of Free Emissions Allowances under EPA's Clean Power Plan*. Discussion Paper No. 16-20. Washington, DC: Resources for the Future.

Burtraw, D., Palmer, K., Munnings, C., Weber, P., Woerman, M., 2013. *Linking by Degrees: Incremental Alignment of Cap-and-Trade Markets*. Discussion Paper No. 13-04. Washington, DC: Resources for the Future.

Bussmann, K.-D., 2020. *Detecting Money Laundering in Emissions Trading*. Dessau-Roßlau: Federal Environmental Agency.

CDM Accreditation Panel, 2008. *Twenty-Sixth Progress Report of the CDM Accreditation Panel*. Bonn.

CDM Executive Board, 2011a. *Final Ruling Regarding the Request for Issuance of CERs "Aquarius Hydroelectric Project" (0627)*. Bonn.

CDM Executive Board, 2011b. *Final Ruling Regarding the Request for Issuance of CERs of "Bundled Wind Power Project in Chitradurga (Karnataka in India) Managed by Enercon (India) Ltd" (0276)*. Bonn.

Chen, H., Letmathe, P., Soderstrom, N., 2021. Reporting bias and monitoring in Clean Development Mechanism projects. *Contemporary Accounting Research*, 38, 7–31.

Clò, S., 2009. The effectiveness of the EU emissions trading scheme. *Climate Policy*, 9(3), 227–241.

Cludius, J., 2018. Winners and losers of EU emissions trading: Insights from the EUTL transfer dataset. *Economics of Energy & Environmental Policy*, 7(2), 93–110.

Cludius, J., Betz, R., 2020. The role of banks in EU emission trading. *The Energy Journal*, 41(2), 275–299.

de Sepibus, J., 2007a. *The European Emission Trading Scheme Put to the Test of State Aid Rules*. NCCR Trade Regulation Working Paper No. 2007/34. Bern: World Trade Institute.

de Sepibus, J., 2007b. *Scarcity and Allocation of Allowances in the EU Emissions Trading Scheme – A Legal Analysis.* NCCR Trade Regulation Working Paper No. 2007/32. Bern: World Trade Institute.

Di Santo, D., De Chicchis, L., Biele, E., 2018. White certificates in Italy: Lessons learnt over 12 years of evaluation. In *2018 International Energy Policy & Programme Evaluation Conference.* Vienna.

Dobson, R., 2015. *Carbon Market Corruption Risks and Mitigation Strategies.* Berlin: Transparency International.

Drew, J., Drew, M., 2010. Establishing additionality: Fraud vulnerabilities in the Clean Development Mechanism. *Accounting Research Journal,* 23, 243–253.

Dworkin, R. M., 1978. *Taking Rights Seriously.* London: Duckworth.

European Commission (EC), 2015. *Carbon Market Report 2015.* Brussels.

European Commission (EC), 2021. *Commission Staff Working Document Accompanying the Report from the Commission to the European Parliament and the Council on the Functioning of the European Carbon Market in 2020.* Brussels. https://ec.europa.eu/clima/system/files/2021-10/swd_2021_308_en.pdf.

European Court of Auditors (ECA), 2015. *Special Report: The Integrity and Implementation of the EU ETS.* Luxembourg. www.eca.europa.eu/Lists/ECADocuments/SR15_06/SR15_06_EN.pdf.

Europol, 2009. *Carbon Credit Fraud Causes More Than 5 Billion Euros Damage for European Taxpayer.* The Hague. www.europol.europa.eu/newsroom/news/carbon-credit-fraud-causes-more-5-billion-euros-damage-for-european-taxpayer.

Frunza, M.-C., Guegan, D., Lassoudiere, A., 2011. Missing trader fraud on the emissions market. *Journal of Financial Crime,* 18(2), 183–194.

Gold Standard, 2021. *Treatment of Double Counting and Corresponding Adjustments in Voluntary Carbon Markets.* Geneva. www.goldstandard.org/sites/default/files/documents/gs_guidance_correspondingadjustments_feb2021.pdf.

Green, J. F., Sterner, T., Wagner, G., 2014. A balance of bottom-up and top-down in linking climate policies. *Nature Climate Change,* 4(12), 1064–1067.

Greiner, S., Michaelowa, A., 2003. Defining investment additionality for CDM projects – practical approaches. *Energy Policy,* 31, 1007–1015.

Grubb, M., Ferrario, F., 2006. False confidences: Forecasting errors and emission caps in CO_2 trading systems. *Climate Policy,* 6, 495–501.

Grumbach, J., 2015. Polluting industries as climate protagonists: Cap-and-trade and the problem of business preferences. *Business and Politics,* 17(4), 633–659.

Gulbrandsen, L. H., Wettestad, J., Victor, D. G., Underdal, A., 2019. The political roots of divergence in carbon market design: Implications for linking. *Climate Policy*, 19(4), 427–438.

Gupta, S., Tirpak, D., Burger, N. et al., 2007. Policies, instruments and co-operative arrangements. In B. Metz, O. R. Davidson, P. R. Bosch, R. Dave and L. A. Meyer (Eds.), *Climate Change 2007: Mitigation. Contribution of Working Group III to the Fourth Assessment Report of the Intergovernmental Panel on Climate Change.* Cambridge: Cambridge University Press, 746–807.

Hahn, R. W., 1984. Market power and transferable property rights. *The Quarterly Journal of Economics*, 99(4), 753–765.

Hahn, R. W., Stavins, R. N., 2011. The effect of allowance allocations on cap-and-trade system performance. *The Journal of Law and Economics*, 54 (S4), 267–294.

Haites, E., 2016. Experience with linking greenhouse gas emissions trading systems. *WIREs Energy Environment*, 5(3), 246–260.

Haites, E., 2018. Carbon taxes and greenhouse gas emissions trading systems: What have we learned? *Climate Policy*, 18(8), 955–966.

Hayashi, D., Michaelowa, A., 2013. Standardization of baseline and additionality determination under the CDM. *Climate Policy*, 13(2), 191–209.

Hepburn, C., Grubb, M., Neuhoff, K., Matthes, F., Tse, M., 2006. Auctioning of EU ETS phase II allowances – how and why? *Climate Policy*, 6(1), 137–160.

Hintermann, B., 2016. Emissions trading and market manipulation. In S. E. Weishaar (Eds.), *Research Handbook on Emissions Trading.* Cheltenham: Edward Elgar, 89–110.

Hintermann, B., 2017. Market power in emission permit markets: Theory and evidence from the EU ETS. *Environmental and Resource Economics*, 66(1), 89–112.

Holland, S. P., Moore, M. R., 2012. When to pollute, when to abate? Intertemporal permit use in the Los Angeles NOx market. *Land Economics*, 88(2), 275–299.

Intergovernmental Panel on Climate Change (IPCC) , 2018. *Global Warming of 1.5°C, an IPCC Special Report on the Impacts of Global Warming of 1.5◦C Above Pre-Industrial Levels and Related Global Greenhouse Gas Emission Pathways, in the Context of Strengthening the Global Response to the Threat of Climate Change, Sustainable Development, and Efforts to Eradicate Poverty.* Geneva.

International Carbon Action Partnership (ICAP), 2021. *Emissions Trading Worldwide: Status Report 2021* (2nd Ed.). Berlin.

International Carbon Reduction & Offset Alliance (ICROA), 2020. *ICROA's Position on Scaling Private Sector Voluntary Action Post-2020*. Geneva.

International Criminal Police Organization (INTERPOL), 2013. *Guide to Carbon Trading Crime*. Lyon.

International Energy Agency (IEA), 2021. *Net Zero by 2050*. Paris.

Jarrow, R. A., 1992. Market manipulation, bubbles, corners, and short squeezes. *The Journal of Financial and Quantitative Analysis*, 27(3), 311–336.

Jevnaker, T., Wettestad, J., 2017. Ratcheting up carbon trade: The politics of reforming EU emissions trading. *Global Environmental Politics*, 17(2), 105–124.

Jordan, A., Huitema, D., van Asselt, H., Forster, J., 2018. Governing climate change: The promise and limits of polycentric governance. In A. Jordan, D. Huitema, H. van Asselt and J. Forster (Eds.), *Governing Climate Change: Polycentricity in Action?* Cambridge: Cambridge University Press, 359–383.

Kachi, A., Frerk, M., 2013. *Carbon Market Oversight Primer*. Berlin: International Carbon Action Partnership.

Keppler, J. H., Cruciani, M., 2010. Rents in the European power sector due to carbon trading. *Energy Policy*, 38(8), 4280–4290.

Knox-Hayes, J., 2016. *The Cultures of Markets: The Political Economy of Climate Governance*. Oxford: Oxford University Press.

Kogels, H., 2010. VAT fraud with emission allowances trading. *EC Tax Review*, 19(5), 186–187.

Kohen, M., Schramm, B., 2013. General principles of law. In A. Carty (Ed.), *Oxford Bibliographies in International Law*. Oxford: Oxford University Press. https://doi.org/10.1093/OBO/9780199796953-0063

Kollmuss, A., Schneider, L., Zhezherin, V., 2015. *Has Joint Implementation Reduced GHG Emissions? Lessons Learned for the Design of Carbon Market Mechanisms*. SEI Working Paper No. 2015-07. Stockholm: Stockholm Environment Institute.

Kotsch, R., Betz, R., Abrell, J., Schwendner, P., 2021. The end of the Kyoto Protocol era: What can we learn from the global trade of Emissions Reduction Units applying network analysis? In *26th Annual Conference of the European Association of Environmental and Resource Economists*. Berlin.

Leining, C., Kerr, S., Bruce-Brand, B., 2020. The New Zealand emissions trading scheme: Critical review and future outlook for three design innovations. *Climate Policy*, 20(2), 246–264.

Liski, M., Montero, J.-P., 2011. Market power in an exhaustible resource market: The case of storable pollution permits. *The Economic Journal*, 121 (551), 116–144.

Lunt, M. F., Rigby, M., Ganesan, A. L. et al., 2015. Reconciling reported and unreported HFC emissions with atmospheric observations. *Proceedings of the National Academy of Sciences of the United States of America*, 112(19), 5927–5931.

Markussen, P., Svendsen, G. T., 2005. Industry lobbying and the political economy of GHG trade in the European Union. *Energy Policy*, 33(2), 245–255.

Mate, N., Ghosh, S., 2009. The Jindal CDM projects in Karnataka. In S. Böhm and S. Dabhi (Eds.), *Upsetting the Offset*. London: MayFly Books, 148–150.

McAllister, L. K., 2010. The enforcement challenge of cap-and-trade regulation. *Environmental Law*, 40(4), 1195–1230.

Meng, K. C., Rode, A., 2019. The social cost of lobbying over climate policy. *Nature Climate Change*, 9, 472–476.

Meng, T., 2013. *Study on Plant Load Factor of Wind Power CDM Projects*. Master Thesis in Sustainable Development, No. 151, Department of Earth Sciences. Uppsala: Uppsala University.

Michaelowa, A., 2005. Determination of baselines and additionality for the CDM: A crucial element of credibility of the climate regime. In F. Yamin (Ed.), *Climate Change and Carbon Markets: A Handbook of Emission Reduction Mechanisms*. London: Earthscan, 305–320.

Michaelowa, A., 2007. *Additionality Determination of Indian CDM Projects: Can Indian CDM Project Developers Outwit the CDM Executive Board?* Discussion Paper No. CDM-1. London: Climate Strategies.

Michaelowa, A., 2009. Interpreting the additionality of CDM projects: Changes in additionality definitions and regulatory practices over time. In D. Freestone and C. Streck (Eds.), *Legal Aspects of Carbon Trading*. Oxford: Oxford University Press, 248–271.

Michaelowa, A., 2021. COP26 summary, presentation held on December 8, 2021, in a webinar by Perspectives Climate Group.

Michaelowa, A., Brescia, D., Wohlgemuth, N. et al., 2020a. *CDM Method Transformation: Updating and Transforming CDM Methods for Use in an Article 6 Context*. Freiburg: Perspectives Climate Change.

Michaelowa, A., Buen, J., 2012. The CDM gold rush. In A. Michaelowa (Ed.), *Carbon Markets or Climate Finance?* Abingdon: Routledge, 1–38.

Michaelowa, A., Censkowsky, P., Espelage, A. et al., 2021a. *Volumes and Types of Unused Certified Emission Reductions (CERs) – Lessons Learned from CDM Transactions under the Kyoto Protocol, Transparency Gaps and Implications for Post-2020 International Carbon Markets*. Freiburg: Perspectives Climate Change.

Michaelowa, A., Espelage, A., 't Gilde, L., Chagas, T., 2020b. *Promoting Transparency in Article 6: Designing a Coherent and Robust Reporting and Review Cycle in the Context of Operationalising Articles 6 and 13 of the Paris Agreement*. Freiburg: Perspectives Climate Change.

Michaelowa, A., Hermwille, L., Obergassel, W., Butzengeiger, S., 2019a. Additionality revisited: Guarding the integrity of market mechanisms under the Paris Agreement. *Climate Policy*, 19, 1211–1224.

Michaelowa, A., Michaelowa, K., Hermwille, L., Espelage, A., 2021b. *Towards Net Zero: Dynamic Baselines for International Market Mechanisms*. CIS Working Paper No. 107. Zurich: Center for Comparative and International Studies.

Michaelowa, A., Shishlov, I., Bofill, P., Hoch, S., Espelage, A., 2019b. *Overview and Comparison of Existing Carbon Crediting Schemes*. Helsinki: Nordic Environment Finance Corporation (NEFCO).

Michaelowa, A., Shishlov, I., Brescia, D., 2019c. Evolution of international carbon markets: Lessons for the Paris Agreement. *Wiley Interdisciplinary Reviews: Climate Change*, 10(6), e613. https://doi.org/10.1002/wcc.613.

Michaelowa, K., Michaelowa, A., 2017. The growing influence of the UNFCCC secretariat on the Clean Development Mechanism. *International Environmental Agreements*, 17(2), 247–269.

Morris, D., 2012. *Losing the Lead? Europe's Flagging Carbon Market. The 2012 Environmental Outlook for the EU ETS*. London: Sandbag.

Muñiz, J. R.-T., 1997. Legal principles and legal theory. *Ratio Juris*, 10(3), 267–287.

Neuhoff, K., Acworth, W., Ismer, R., Sartor, O., Zetterberg, L., 2015. Leakage protection for carbon-intensive materials post-2020. *DIW Economic Bulletin*, 5(28/29), 397–404.

Neuhoff, K., Åhman, M., Betz, R. et al., 2006. Implications of announced phase II national allocation plans for the EU ETS. *Climate Policy*, 6(4), 411–422.

Neuhoff, K., Schopp, A., Boyd, R., Stelmakh, K., Vasa, A., 2012. *Banking of Surplus Emissions Allowances: Does the Volume Matter?* DIW Berlin Discussion Paper No. 1196. Berlin: Deutsches Institut für Wirtschaftsforschung.

Nguyen, N. T., Ha-Duong, M., Greiner, S., Mehling, M., 2011. Implementing the Clean Development Mechanism in Vietnam: Potential and limitations. In M. Mehling, A. Merill and K. Upston-Hooper (Eds.), *Improving the Clean Development Mechanism: Options and Challenges Post-2012*. Berlin: Lexxion, 221–246.

Nield, K., Pereira, R., 2016. Financial crimes in the European carbon markets. In S. E. Weishaar (Ed.), *Research Handbook on Emissions Trading*. Cheltenham: Edward Elgar, 195–231.

Oberndorfer, U., 2009. EU emission allowances and the stock market: Evidence from the electricity industry. *Ecological Economics*, 68(4), 1116–1126.

Partnership for Market Readiness (PMR), International Carbon Action Partnership (ICAP), 2021. *Emissions Trading in Practice: A Handbook on Design and Implementation*. Washington, DC: World Bank.

Paterson, M., Hoffmann, M., Betsill, M., Bernstein, S., 2014. The micro-foundations of policy diffusion toward complex global governance. *Comparative Political Studies*, 47(3), 420–449.

Pattberg, P., Stripple, J., 2008. Beyond the public and private divide: Remapping transnational climate governance in the 21st century. *International Environmental Agreements: Politics, Law and Economics*, 8 (4), 367–388.

Pauw, W. P., Cassanmagnano, D., Mbeva, K. et al., 2016. *NDC Explorer*. Bonn, Nairobi, Stockholm: German Development Institute, African Centre for Technology Studies, Stockholm Environment Institute.

Payne, C. R., 2017. Defining the environment: Environmental integrity. In C. Stahn, J. Iverson and J. S. Easterday (Eds.), *Environmental Protection and Transitions from Conflict to Peace: Clarifying Norms, Principles, and Practices*. Oxford: Oxford University Press, 40–70.

Pearse, R., 2016. The coal question that emissions trading has not answered. *Energy Policy*, 99, 319–328.

Perspectives Climate Group, 2022. *Launch of International Initiative for Development of Article 6 Methodology Tools (II-AMT)*. Freiburg.www .perspectives.cc/public/fileadmin/user_upload/Art_6_Tools_Press_Release_-_ 2_pages.pdf.

Rosendahl, K., Strand, J., 2009. *Simple Model Frameworks for Explaining Inefficiency of the Clean Development Mechanism*. Policy Research Working Paper No. 4931. Washington, DC: World Bank.

Sartor, O., Pallière, C., Lecourt, S., 2014. Benchmark-based allocation in EU ETS Phase 3: An early assessment. *Climate Policy*, 14, 507–524.

Sartzetakis, E. S., 1997. Tradeable emission permits regulations in the presence of imperfectly competitive product markets: Welfare implications. *Environmental and Resource Economics*, 9(1), 65–81.

Schneider, L., 2009. Assessing the additionality of CDM projects: Practical experiences and lessons learned. *Climate Policy*, 9, 242–254.

Schneider, L., 2011. Perverse incentives under the CDM: An evaluation of HFC-23 destruction projects. *Climate Policy*, 11, 851–864.

Schneider, L., Duan, M., Stavins, R. et al., 2019. Double counting and the Paris Agreement rulebook. *Science*, 366(6462), 180–183.

Schneider, L., Kollmuss, A., Lazarus, M., 2015. Addressing the risk of double counting emission reductions under the UNFCCC. *Climatic Change*, 131(4), 473–486.

Schneider, L., La Hoz Theuer, S., 2019. Environmental integrity of international carbon market mechanisms under the Paris Agreement. *Climate Policy*, 19 (3), 386–400.

Schneider, L., Mohr, L., 2010. *2010 Rating of Designated Operational Entities (DOEs) Accredited under the Clean Development Mechanism (CDM)*. Report for WWF. Berlin: Öko-Institut.

Schumacher, N., 2020. Die Pflicht zur Abgabe von Emissionsberechtigungen bei insolventen Betreibern im Emissionshandel. *Zeitschrift für das gesamte Insolvenz- und Sanierungsrecht*, 37, 1916–1922.

Shen, P., Betz, R., Ortmann, A., Gong, R., 2020. Improving truthful reporting of polluting firms by rotating inspectors: Experimental evidence from a bribery game. *Environmental and Resource Economics*, 76(2–3), 201–233.

Sijm, J., Neuhof, K., Chen, Y., 2006. CO_2 cost pass-through and windfall profits in the power sector. *Climate Policy*, 6, 49–72.

Stavins, R., Zou, J., Brewer, T. et al., 2014. International cooperation: Agreements and instruments. In O. Edenhofer, R. Pichs-Madruga, Y. Sokona et al. (Eds.), *Climate Change 2014: Mitigation of Climate Change. Contribution of Working Group III to the Fifth Assessment Report of the Intergovernmental Panel on Climate Change*. Cambridge: Cambridge University Press, 1001–1082.

Strand, J., Rosendahl, K., 2012. Global emissions effects of CDM projects with relative baselines. *Resource and Energy Economics*, 34, 533–548.

Stranlund, J., Murphy, J., Spraggon, J., 2011. An experimental analysis of compliance in dynamic emissions markets. *Journal of Environmental Economics and Management*, 62, 414–429.

Verde, S., Teixidó, J., Marcantonini, C., Labandeira, X., 2018. Free allocation rules in the EU emissions trading system – what does the empirical literature show? *Climate Policy*, 19(4), 439–452.

Wei, X., 2016. *Three Essays on Carbon and Environmental Markets in the EU and China*. PhD Thesis, School of Economics, UNSW Business School. Sydney: University of New South Wales.

Wettestad, J., 2009. Interaction between EU carbon trading and the international climate regime: Synergies and learning. *International Environmental Agreements: Politics, Law and Economics*, 9(4), 393–408.

Wettestad, J., Gulbrandsen, L. H., 2018. *The Evolution of Carbon Markets: Design and Diffusion*. Abingdon: Routledge.

Wettestad, J., Jevnaker, T., 2016. *Rescuing EU Emissions Trading*. London: Palgrave Macmillan.

Wettestad, J., Jevnaker, T., 2019. Smokescreen politics? Ratcheting up EU emissions trading in 2017. *Review of Policy Research*, 36(5), 635–659.

Williams, C. C., 2013. A burning desire: The need for anti-money laundering regulations in carbon emissions trading schemes to combat emerging criminal typologies. *Journal of Money Laundering Control*, 16(4), 298–320.

Wood, B., Sallu, S., Paavola, J., 2016. Can CDM finance energy access in least developed countries? Evidence from Tanzania. *Climate Policy*, 16, 456–473.

World Bank, 2021. *State and Trends of Carbon Pricing 2021*. Washington, DC.

Zhang, H., Boute, A., Acworth, W., 2021. *China's Pilot Emissions Trading Systems and Electricity Markets (Hubei and Shenzhen) – Influence of Market Structures and Market Regulations on the Carbon Market*. Dessau-Roßlau: Federal Environmental Agency.

Acknowledgement

The authors gratefully acknowledge financial support by the Swiss Network for International Studies (SNIS) in the framework of the project "Designing Effective Regulation for Carbon Markets at the International, National and Regional Level", which enabled this publication.

Cambridge Elements

Earth System Governance

Frank Biermann
Utrecht University

Frank Biermann is Research Professor of Global Sustainability Governance with the Copernicus Institute of Sustainable Development, Utrecht University, the Netherlands. He is the founding Chair of the Earth System Governance Project, a global transdisciplinary research network launched in 2009; and Editor-in-Chief of the new peer-reviewed journal *Earth System Governance* (Elsevier). In April 2018, he won a European Research Council Advanced Grant for a research program on the steering effects of the Sustainable Development Goals.

Aarti Gupta
Wageningen University

Aarti Gupta is Professor of Global Environmental Governance at Wageningen University, The Netherlands. She is Lead Faculty and a member of the Scientific Steering Committee of the Earth System Governance (ESG) Project and a Coordinating Lead Author of its 2018 Science and Implementation Plan. She is also principal investigator of the Dutch Research Council-funded TRANSGOV project on the Transformative Potential of Transparency in Climate Governance. She holds a PhD from Yale University in environmental studies.

Michael Mason
London School of Economics and Political Science (LSE)

Michael Mason is Associate Professor in the Department of Geography and Environment at the London School of Economics and Political Science (LSE). At LSE he also Director of the Middle East Centre and an Associate of the Grantham Institute on Climate Change and the Environment. Alongside his academic research on environmental politics and governance, he has advised various governments and international organisations on environmental policy issues, including the European Commission, ICRC, NATO, the UK Government (FCDO) and UNDP.

About the Series

Linked with the Earth System Governance Project, this exciting new series will provide concise but authoritative studies of the governance of complex socio-ecological systems, written by world-leading scholars. Highly interdisciplinary in scope, the series will address governance processes and institutions at all levels of decision-making, from local to global, within a planetary perspective that seeks to align current institutions and governance systems with the fundamental 21st Century challenges of global environmental change and earth system transformations.
Elements in this series will present cutting edge scientific research, while also seeking to contribute innovative transformative ideas towards better governance. A key aim of the series is to present policy-relevant research that is of interest to both academics and policy-makers working on earth system governance.
More information about the Earth System Governance project can be found at: www.earthsystemgovernance.org.

Cambridge Elements ≡

Earth System Governance

Printed in the United States
by Baker & Taylor Publisher Services